CONNIVING COMMUNICATION

Attention Authors

Manas Publications is fighting a war to tell the world that India can win the battle not only by the bullet but also by pen. We are converting fighters into writers. There is no dearth of intellectuals in our country, however, their knowledge is confined to them only. No sincere effort has been made by any other publisher to channelise their knowledge, that is why the talent of maximum intellectuals remains latent. An author always presents the raw material in the shape of a manuscript and it is the job of the publisher to convert it into a finished product. Manas has been continually motivating intellectuals and publishing their manuscripts for more than two decades and would like to publish your manuscript too. If you or your colleagues have a manuscript ready for publication or are working on it, contact us with a detailed synopsis and list of contents. Manas can also suggest you a suitable title for writing related to your area of expertise. Manas is known for its publishing quality. We take utmost care in publishing and also give wide publicity to the book and its author through our national and international distribution network.

CONNIVING COMMUNICATION

Brig MS Jaswal

Manas Publications
(We Convert Fighters into Writers)
New Delhi-110002 (INDIA)

MANAS PUBLICATIONS
(Publishers, Distributors, Importers & Exporters)
4402/5-A, Ansari Road (Opp. HDFC Bank)
Darya Ganj, New Delhi-110 002 (INDIA)
Off. ✆ 23260783, 23265523, Res. ✆ 23842660
Fax: 011-23272766
E-mail: manaspublications@vsnl.com
manaspublications@gmail.com
www.manaspublications.in

ISBN 978-81-7049-383-9
Rs. 495

Typeset at
Manas Publications

Printed in India at
RK Print Services, Delhi
and published by Mrs Suman Lata for
Manas Publications, 4402/5-A, Ansari Road
(Opp. HDFC Bank),
Darya Ganj, New Delhi-110 002 (INDIA)

Contents

The Devotion

I dedicate this book to my younger son Somendra, who keeps me on my toes due to his communication demands and all those dear friends with whom I could never communicate in total honesty and display the purity of my intent. To them I do apologise.

Author's Note

The dawn of human race, in its full glory and grace can be attributed to the dogged determination of our basic building blocks, the genes, to communicate with the environment and survive. Had they not connived with the nature to adapt and move forward in their journey of life, we surely would not have been here.

The idea to write on communications germinated when I was interacting with various people to write my previous military fiction books, *Crimson Kashmir, Kargil Knot* and *Timed Out* my first foray into management.

My quest to understanding this unique phenomenon has increased manifold as I embarked upon this mundane exercise about two years back to pen my views on a simple aspect as I so wrongly perceived about communication. Each journey opened up new horizons which only astounded me. In fact, I am humbled at the vastness of the subject and still grasping with its totality.

In the end I can only say the following—

"You can only decide,

On which communication plane to glide.

If you decide to deride,

You will surely miss an exciting ride,

It's like a shining asteroid,

Ban it and live a life of void".

Preface

> We do not choose to be born. We do not choose our parents. We do not choose our historical epoch, or the country of our birth, nor the immediate circumstances of our upbringing. Neither we choose to die, nor do we choose the time or circumstances of our death. However, we do choose our mode of living—to live courageously, or cowardly, honourably or dishonourably, with purpose or adrift. We decide what is important and what is trivial in life. We decide that what makes us significant is either what we do or what we refuse to do. Nevertheless, no matter how indifferent the universe is to our choices and decisions, these choices and decisions are ours to make. We decide. We lay the road map out of our life.
>
> – **Joseph Epstein,**
> *Ambition the Secret Passion,* page 298.

This is my second foray into aspects of management. I love all those aspects of management, which affects our lives. The first book, 'Timed Out' was for managing your time better. This one I want to devote in making effective communication. Communication, I believe, is the bedrock on which shapes our relationships with the community and near ones. Without communication, we are inanimate.

Whatever issue affects our lives makes an interesting subject to narrate. However, when one glances on this aspect of communication, many a researcher has tabulated their love on this sole score to reach fame and fortune. Then why a puny, unknown man like me, again wants to tread places touched already by so many.

Maybe, I am a born egoist who thinks others before me were not as understanding as they should have been. Maybe, the others have touched the subject with so many technicalities that an idiot in me does not understand them, as one should. Maybe, they have not touched my heart, as they should have. Maybe, I want to tell a different story. Maybe, my ideas are different and so is the mode of narration. Be that may, I intend to narrate my reflections.

When I first expressed my intention to my juniors at my workplace, they were flabbergasted on two counts: one; why this subject, which has authentic books aplenty two; why a word 'Conniving', which has perceivably a negative connotation for such a positive intent as communication. They were right in their own perception of things.

You think what you say is pure in intent and make no demands. We know any communication makes demands. When you make demand, its fulfillment is a very complex task. It involves human mind, which thinks of million permutations and combinations a second and how to fulfill that demand by least application of energy, time and resources, within the rationality of individual brain. You involve a group, then the issue becomes that more complex, as re-communicating to find execution harmony to one demand is not a natural process of agreement but antithesis to human behaviour of individuality. When you select a response, you are conniving with set of choices to choose the best. Similarly, when you make a demand, you are conniving with the mental faculty of another individual or an association of individuals to impel them to do what you want them to do.

Let me explain my hypothesis a bit further, with the help of four examples:

- When do you communicate with God? When things do not go right for you or you are in extreme difficulties. You want something from God. I feel you are conniving to obtain his blessings. When you pray to God for the happiness, I feel that you are conniving to obtain his uninterrupted blessings that no ill-omen befalls you or your family. When you pray to thank him, you are asking for his connived blessings of goodness and large heartedness.
- When your boss orders you to do a task, he is conniving with your natural lethargy and mind rebellion to get you to do the work as per his desires. If the work were already complete, the boss would have never told you to do so in the first place. However, work never seems to be ending, suggesting that the subordinate is never thinking ahead/working and thus the boss goads him repeatedly.
- When your child smiles at you and asks for his quota of daily sweets, he or she is craving your love to enable you to do just that. In addition, when they smile for just love of it they are conniving to get a smile in return. Studies in child behaviour reveal that babies six month old connive and manipulate elders by series of cries, laughter, anger and other emotions to attract attention to gain their desire.
- Are today's students learning from their teachers for the sake of learning? Are the teachers of today imparting knowledge for the inspirational quest of imparting knowledge? Answer obviously is no and it comes from our hearts. All are conniving by using fair or unfair means to achieve their goals. Ends matter, not the means.

Conniving/manipulating is a natural phenomenon, when viewed in its entirety of the system by which people make demands and fulfill their desires.

Let us test this hypothesis on human hunger.

You pursue and kill animals for one source of food. In addition, you grow various varieties of food; engineer them for more productivity for meeting our food requirement. Currently, phenomenal research is going on to evolve new varieties of edibles to keep the stomach of a human always full. What are we essentially doing? Are not we conniving with our food supply chain to keep our tummy's full? Even when a mother is experimenting with various taste requirements of her child, she is conniving with the child's tastes to ensure he is fed well.

Had humans not connived to eat meat and veggies, we would have perished.

Now having learnt about conniving as an art of manipulating emotions, thoughts and actions, do you feel connived always. When I first gave the thought to this aspect, I did feel manipulated by those who I loved the most

Even the latest Russian research brings forth the subject that genes communicate and connive with elements of nature to produce genetic communication and they manipulate their environment for their own best use and mutation. Had they not done that, I am sure we would not have been humans as we see ourselves but some monkeys sitting on top of a tree.

When my wife smiles without a reason at me, I feel connived. My perceptions and mind goes further into overdrive including my apprehensions when my beloved wife smiles for no obvious reason, more than twice in a day. When she repeats the exercise into another day, I am a nervous wreck. When my palpitations become unbearable, I do muster adequate courage to walk up to her and simply ask after clearing a big lump in my throat, "What do you want dear?" Like a guessing magician, I feel happy when prompt comes in the demand.

Communication throws out an intent.

A thrown intent triggers your mind into action. When Lord Krishna was giving discourse to his mind-defeated pupil Arjuna, on the battlefield of Kurukshetra, in the divine book 'Gita', what was his intention to connive? He wanted Arjuna the most avid warrior, to shun inaction and have recourse in taking positive action.

From the state of inaction to the state of action, the communication has to be first understood, its implications on your physical and mental state made clear, then the acceptance of the mind has to repel the natural rebel element of curtailment of freedom and physical state overcome the natural state of lethargy. If acceptance dawns in totality of good intention of the communication then action will result. Have you ever spied on a well-fed sleeping man? If he hears no communication, he keeps on sleeping. Even if he hears his child crying, he ignores it, for right intent was not thrown at him.

With communication, you activate action.

With effective communication, you perform effective action. However, the, resultant action may not be the desired action. My wife's smile for over three days was to stimulate me into action, which would bring her the diamond solitaire she wanted so silly. My reaction to present her with less expensive option of a romantic candle-lit dinner would erase her smile and may invite a slap instead.

The total sum of intentions sum up the entire process of communication.

The process of communication may last a microsecond or an eternity. Until it is not fully satisfactory to the parties involved, they will continue to be in the suspended state of animated communication. I know my wife wants a solitaire. Moreover, I intend buying her a solitaire. However, when? That is a million-dollar question.

Definitely, before my lifetime but then, the old woman may not want to flash her gems along with her false teeth. Ha, so let the communication continue.

I am in a total state of non-communication with both my growing up teenage sons. The elder one understands me and so do I. However, my younger son who is going to be twelve foxes me the most. I dedicate this book to Somendra, my cutest younger one, who I love very much, but we do not see eye to eye on any issue, though he does more parental aping than my elder one. Is it the generation gap or the distance between the mindsets that affects the communication? I think both do and these two issues do play a major part in effective communication.

Communication is the essence of life, as we perceive it.

Imagine a life, devoid off sensory inputs of communication. One can understand the pain of some such special people who are devoid off this God given gift. How do they feel? It will open your eyes when you hear one. What God do they perceive? What good in life they perceive? What feelings have they?

I just wanted to bring a brutal fact to fore that we communication-illiterate perceive speech and hearing as major part of communication. There can be nothing far from reality, as hearing forms only a minuscule part of communication.

Those unfortunate children, who are born deaf and mute, they too are endowed with the faculty of perception. They dream, smile and communicate. They open their other powers of communication, which we have closed. They open their mind much more and we close our mind much more. They use those facets of our own natural ability to communicate which we have closed for the silly reason that we are not aware that it exists. They have more extrasensory perception.

Communication involves complete involvement of all sensory organs.

Besides body language and gestures, communication involves sensory organs such as sense of touch, smell, sight, hearing and speech as well. Human mind plays a significant role in communication.

Telepathy is the highest mode of communication.

Telepathy or paranormal communication is the highest and purest form of communication, for we can foresee a communication demand and act on it positively before putting forward the demand. It is clear in intent and subsequent action.

However, the benefits of telepathy do not come to sleepy fools like us. It is a gift of God. Learned men sacrifice their lifetime to attain it. We little minions at least can try to achieve it. If not telepathy, we can attain some high degree of communication but we have to train ourselves for it. Surprisingly, living species have this gift of wonderful mode of communication and I will focus on the subject hereinafter.

In my entire life, I have felt the perfect telepathy with the woman of my love, twice. Once when she was shopping for an entire day for a friend and on entering the car she said, "I am famished and I want to have Chicken Tikkas." I pointed to the box in front of the dashboard and when she opened it, they were piping hot Chicken Tikkas. Second was when one day she said, "I need Rupees ten thousand to buy my sister a present." I pointed her to her purse and lo and behold, there were Rupees ten thousand in it. In my marriage of seventeen years and this golden moment happened only twice in life. A very sad state of perfect communications at least with a person you declare to love the most. When we are not in a state of telepathy, my beloved wife, and me, are in state of total non-communication. I want an omelette or single fry egg double fried and I get a boiled potato or single fry egg with sunny side up. I wear the best clothes from my closet and she makes me strip down to match her sari mostly or redress properly.

Why blame my wife, it is the same with my children. I want them to get ninety percent marks and they glee in happiness with fifty percent score. I want them to eat most of the meals at home but the dirty roadside vendor only satisfies their hunger pangs. My mother wants me around to help her in old age and she ends up helping her young son. So the travails of ultimate communication, which automatically satisfies everyone, are many and it is for us to find our own right path to communicate effectively.

Most of our lives we live in a state of total non-communication.

We live in the state of non-communication for we do not open our mind. We are also lethargic and assume communication, as we perceive it. The distortion in initial communication overwhelms us so much that we live in the state of non-communication.

Distortion in communication occurs when we close our mind.

In a few cases, the distortion in communication occurs due to the physical break in communication or its clarity. In most cases, distortion occurs in your mind because the way you perceive different situations. Our intentions are not correct sometimes nor do we have the ability to assume responsibility or take risks. We act on expectations of reward or absence of it. All these factors help in communication message not getting through; hence, they become barriers to communication.

My mother, my wife, my both sons and I can sit in a huddle the whole day and despite given a precise set of instructions will perform them differently. For humans perception, intent, expectancy, risk taking etc differs from situation-to-situation and man-to-man. This shapes our action to the given communication.

Age tempers perception.

- Boss and the youngest executive do not think alike.
- Father and son do not think alike.
- Mother and daughter do not think alike.
- Seasoned politician and the fiery young politician do not think alike.
- Old accountant and a new graduate do not think alike.

Age gives you additional wisdom to do things. The old are old; their mindset is outdated yet we seek their advice because they perceive things differently. All humans perceive things differently, as they have learnt to react differently in their life, as their experiences are in variance. Let me explain it a bit further with a few examples.

- Given the same communication, say of a movie, reactions to it are different. You may love the movie while others say it is just fine.
- Given the same scene in the market, you see something, which your wife does not.
- Given a same appreciation, some are happy and some are not.
- Given the same question paper, students answer it differently.

Acquired knowledge, your experiences, religious beliefs, the way you were brought up, family and peer circle, your attitude to life, your culture, your imagination, and your thoughts at that precise moment and most importantly, how well you radiate as a communication antenna - all these factors temper our perceptions.

Communication covers all aspects of human body.

It encompasses your sight through eyes, sound through ears, touch through sensors of the skin and all communicate with mind, which interprets and rationalises the communication intent and communicates to other organs how to execute the action.

Communication is all pervasive.

If we are surrounded by communication aura, then it becomes that more important that we study it in a little more detail. Even if we take communication as a matter of vague interest, we should study it in different perspective. It is in what state of communication you found yourself trapped in since your childhood will shape your thought. Happy and understanding parents bring happy and understanding generations to fore.

'Child is the father of man', is not an out of context quote. He learns all the good or bad things he sees or taught as a communication experience throughout his formative years. Father, relearns as a process, how his child reacts to perceived correct or bad behaviour, which manifests from the child's perception of things. The cycle of learning and relearning, through continuous communication, is continuous. Parental aping is one of the quickest ways a child learns as values, good or bad, for interaction in society.

Communication and understanding of it shape human behaviour.

Communication shapes your character. When I mused over this thought that communication had shaped my character, I wanted to gauge how much effect my parent's communication had on me especially after I had become a man of my own independent thoughts and had shaped my life independent of them. I was astounded to rediscover on self-actualisation that my parents had moulded more than seventy percent of my character.

Largely, I am what my parents were. Their good parental communication has moulded me into what I am. Some people are the stark opposites of their parents, rebel and if analysed are complete reversal of their parents. Why is that so? Was their parental communication so offensive that they did not even want a part of it in their actual lives? It is so unacceptable for them to imbibe the parental guiding communication.

What an unborn child learns through communication in the womb of his mother also shapes how you behave at least until first two years of your life. We know from the Indian mythology that Abhimanyu learnt the knowledge of entering the 'chakravhayu' in the womb of his mother, when her husband narrated the tale. My elder son would suddenly become calm-quite from his cranky best, as a toddler, when we would put on Don Williams country music, as it was what my wife used to hear when she was expecting him.

Communication does not only shape your life it controls your behaviour.

How your initial contact with the environment went (parents, friends, and society) will be the way you will behave at home in private or out with friends in public. Your aggression, quiet solitude, boisterousness, introvert/ extrovert behaviour will be guide by that first lessons you concluded from your first or subsequent contacts.

I also wanted to touch on a very important issue regarding communication. Continuous or sometimes the first communication is as an essence as how you perceive another person. He is intelligent, handsome, beautiful, tactful, attentive, hardworking etc can all be summed up in first or subsequent sight.

Communication shapes relationships.

My father a very calm man instilled very early in my life that only dogs fight and men resolve differences. We resolve differences through our reasoning power tempered by communication. When both parties stop communication, it severs relationships. What is a divorce or a bad fight: bad communication? It shapes how your family will stay together or part. It will tell how your children will help their parents or not. It tells whether the business partners will remain together or part fighting like mad dogs.

What I plan to narrate again may not be stumping or not told earlier in some other form. These are again my very own observations. They are not scientific treatises but what I perceive about the whole gamut of communication. I leave it to the inner beatings of your heart to dwell in this book.

Chapter - 1

Essentials of Communication

"Laws are essential emanations from the self-poised character of God; they radiate from Sun to the circling edge of creation. Verily, the Mighty Lawgiver hath subjected himself unto laws".

—*Theodore Roosevelt*

As always, I leave the most important chapter the shortest. It is just to throw a point that if it does not make any positive meaning to you, then, futility is certain of going through the book. For me to understand communication and all its combined aspects, you have to believe in the following essentials, as enumerated below in four major thoughts.

1. **Communication Inhabits the Mind:** Genesis of the original communication starts in the inner portals of your mind (brain) and after completing its external journey it finishes in the mind and deemed complete only after the completion of the communication action. The mind has to be sated in the end or communication will never be complete.
2. **Communication is Intrinsic to Human Nature:** Communication is the bedrock on which the humans and societies have developed. Without it, there would not have been the world we see today.
3. **Communication engulfs entire Human Body:** We know mind is the boss and if technically put in today's jargon the central processing unit. The

entire body absorbs the communication. The entire body radiates communication.

4. **Communication shapes your Life:** Form the womb to tomb; it is the direct effect of various forms of communication, which gives you the reasoning and knowledge to do what you want to do. What you do, takes you on positive or negative path in life. Hence, in life what you are is what communication you have imbibed.

I have tried to bring the most crucial aspects of communication, which should tease your mind positively. If they do not then, I am not in the same communication plane as you are. You better not communicate with the book or thoughts reflected and find the person with you can communicate.

Chapter - 2

Do You Radiate?

"If you see good in people, you radiate a harmonious loving energy which uplifts those who are around you. If you can maintain this habit, this energy will turn into steady flow as love".

—Annamalai Swami

Do not label me as downright silly because of the heading I have so insensibly chosen. Any object, which absorbs energy in whatever form, also radiates it. It is the universal laws of physics and you cannot be wrong in that.

When you have the ability to absorb radiations of communications, you also have the ability to radiate communication.

- In addition, humans have very big antennæ.
- These antennæ radiate and absorb communications.
- The whole world communicates.
- All humans communicate. I only said so previously. That is what shapes their lives.

Even insects, bees, smart or dumb animals communicate. I do not know if ants have vocal cords or not but was spellbound by the National Geographic documentary of their abilities to communicate. In their intricate labyrinthine anthills, millions of ants pass precise instructions to their brethren, of food, of water, of threats, of work division. They literarily work as an army to let their anthill community thrive and it thrives due to their ability to communicate.

When you radiate communication, you announce your presence to the entire world. When you radiate communication, you seek out others. No one radiates without seeking out others or for just the fun of it.

Communities built over ages centred on those first few families who could communicate and understand each other. From a cluster of two houses, they attracted thousands to build a town or a city. The initial build up into a city was because a few who mattered initially were in communication harmony with others. Later to iron out the disharmonies in communications the society chose clan leaders, kings and when the issues became more complex, then came the adjudicators, to ensure communication between uncommunicative parties.

Why out of ten men left alone in a jungle eight decide to stay together.

It could be out of fear, the need of being with each other, the safety in numbers or anything conceivable. Eight stay together because they can communicate their desires, wants, fears, have a common platform to voice, and listen. They just vibe together better or we can say they communicate amongst themselves better. The two who broke from the group, vibe amongst themselves better and do not vibe with other eight of the group.

On these issues of community and individuals, which make the communities, I have my own observations on them as follows:-

- Individuals stick together if they are in communication harmony.
- Families in communication harmony prefer to stay together to form initial communities.
- Smaller communities have better communication harmony amongst themselves.
- Larger communities invariably have more communication disharmonies.

- Communication disharmony leads to conflicts.
- Communication disharmonies need specialists to resolve.

Let us transpose the same issue of effective communication, from a community to the first formation of a commune living, the family. Which families stick together? Which families have better love and understanding for each other? Which families radiate happiness and love? In the families where individuals bark at each other than talk, are happy or sad? In which families people separate or display animosity.

- Families, which have better communication, radiate love and happiness.
- In a family where the patriarch radiates positive communication, live in harmony of peace and prosperity.
- Where there is no communication harmony, the families break.

Radiating positive communication can only happen when you are a good medium of radiation.

What you must have noticed one unique thing about great leaders, inspiring teachers, spellbinding orators, good doctors and spiritual seers that they are good at communication and radiation. Without these attributes, they would not have been so. Many spiritual teachers also produce such visible balls or columns of light in deep meditation or during energy work, which trigger decidedly pleasant feelings and do not cause any harm. Apparently, this is also dependent on some inner order, quality and origin of the vacuum domain. There are some spiritual teachers, like the young Englishman Ananda, for example, with whom nothing is noticeable at first, but when one tries to take a photograph while they sit and speak or meditate in hyper-communication, one gets only a picture of a white cloud on a chair. Why spiritual leaders have halo around them?

- They have the power to radiate.
- They radiate positive energy.
- They radiate positive communication.
- They maximize each cell, each DNA in their body to radiate in harmony and synchronization.

Humans are radiating antennæ. You radiate communication continuously. However, to radiate good and effective communication the medium of the body has to be a good radiator. Not all humans communicate with same abilities. The person who has better medium radiates better.

Now what could be a good medium to radiate? Pure metals radiate better than adulterated ones. It is same for the humans. Then, if power applied to the radiation will take it across the distance required, the quality of radiation will enable the absorption of radiation by another body.

- **Are we pure?** Here in human antenna it is the purity of the body, in terms of genuineness, altruism, integrity, and intentions.
- **Do we give power to our communication?** How do you boost it? The power here we seek is the strength of knowledge, goodness and truth of the radiation. In reality, same principle applies to normal radio transmitter. More bigger the antenna, more the power (electric) source, more distance the radio signal travels and is more powerful. So why should it be any different for humans who radiate communication energy. It is for you to identify your power source and boost it to maximum.
- **How good is your quality of radiation?** The quality refers to the simplicity, the ease, the cleanliness of the radiation itself. Any clutter in origin or induced through the medium of travel will make the communication ineffective.

The simple fact is that communication is central to everything we do in business. More importantly, your communication skills define your personality. What your supervisors, peers and subordinates think of you is a direct reflection on your communication skills. Being successful, working effectively, getting what you want or need, even how much you enjoy being around your co-workers, the people you spend the maximum of your waking hours with, it is all tied to these all important skills.

The organization I belong to, communication forms the bedrock of moving this lumbering giant of men and material in perfect synchronisation, speed, accuracy to achieve its targets and objectives. I commanded an antiterrorist unit comprising over thousand men. Thousand men came from thousand different places, hundred different organisations and all thousand had thousand different thoughts to do one thing. How could I succeed in achieving what I did? I played the tune on communication and let the magic of its different manifestations deliver my intentions with precision. It did not come easily. You have to train yourself and rise to the occasion and ensure your purity of communication medium remains powerful and true. Few excerpts of my experiences will amplify as we move ahead. Relevant to this narration is that purity of communication was under continuous scrutiny for its intent delivery and effectiveness by regular feedbacks and correcting the anomalies instantly.

Then there is also a very important aspect of honesty of effort. If you do not put effort into the process of communication, you will never be able to communicate effectively. Imagine yourself holed-up in a room and not talking to anyone will you be able to get your message across to your people. Communication requires interaction with humans and not machines. Hence, go out and make an honest effort in meeting and talking to people.

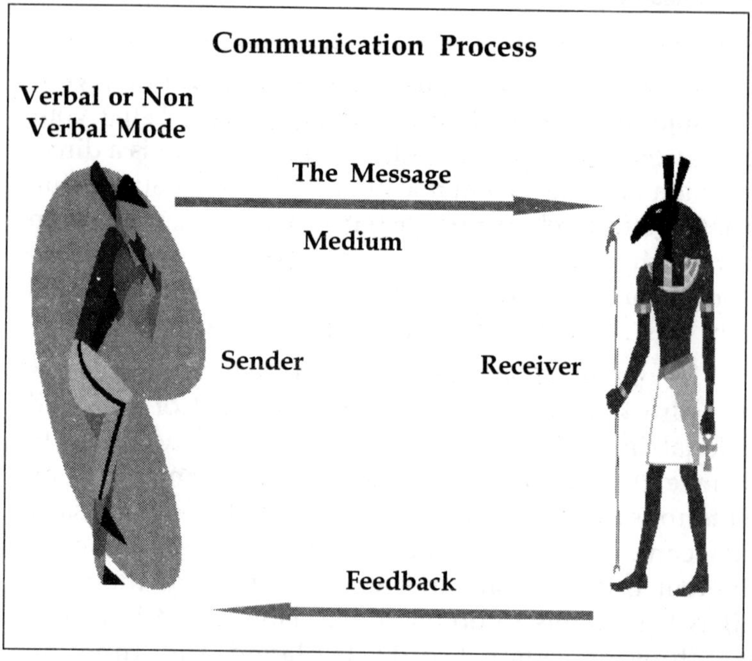

The above diagram illustrates the process of communication in its total entirety. You need a sender, who will send a message through verbal or non-verbal mode, the message itself, which requires a medium to move to the intended target audience, then we need a receiver and lastly the feedback of the message first sent, when received back by the sender, completes the entire process of communication. Thus, the communication process is incomplete unless the communicator sees the resultant action of the original message. This action on receiver's part will subsequently raise further communication if the response was unsatisfactory or cease further communication. Cessation of further communication is also a communication itself to the sender that his action or response was correct. Till the requisite feedback is complied with in totality of satisfying the initial (intent, then only the communication will be said to be camplete).

DO YOU RADIATE?

For knowing your communication abilities we have to undertake another journey to know the various codes by which we radiate communication.

INTERNAL EXPLORATION

- Identify the best communicator in your office, circle of friends and home.
- Identify what are the key factors, which set them apart in the exercise of radiating positive communication.
- Do you feel that you radiate positive communication?

Chapter - 3

Communication Codes

"We must be the epitome - the embodiment of success. We must radiate success before it will come to us. We must first become strong mentally, from an attitude stand point, the people we wish to become".

—Earl Nightingale

I hate the quote above and at the same time love it. I hate it for it tells me to change and I don't want to. I love it for I know change is a continuous process for self betterment. But what is most essential is what we people in life generally are, is how we communicate with the world. The process strangely starts from your genes, mother's womb and later as how you face the society.

We communicate, as we perceive by spoken language.

A language is a syntactically organised system of decipherable signals, such as sounds, modulations or pitch, gestures, posture, facial expressions or written symbols that communicate thoughts or feelings. On that very score of explanation and contrived meaning of what language is all about, all the living species communicate and speak a language. Only place we humans score over them is that they do not have any written script to fall back upon.

Human spoken and written languages (verbal communication) can be described as a system of symbols (sometimes known as lexemes) and the grammar rules by which the symbols are broken and manipulated. The word "language" represents any method of expression or communication; the system of communication used by a particular community or a country. Learning a language is normal in human childhood and a societal cum family pressure. We hear of stories of children left in jungles who developed their own language different from their genetic or societal one. Thus, society forms a very important part in evolution and learning of language. Most human languages use patterns of sound or gesture for symbols, which enable communication with others around them. There are thousands of human languages, and these seem to share common properties.

It is amazing that as the *homo sapiens* across the continents started recognizing the sounds and giving a specific symbol to them, thousands of languages evolved. In contrast, the other species speak the language of their own species. Studies have proved that those races or communities grew and matured faster who had wider range of phonetics and had words to embalm their knowledge as a storage reservoir for future references. In tribal societies that could not evolve their own language to store knowledge, they evolved with lesser pace. However, verbal communication is only seven percent of the whole gamut of communication. Non-verbal communication plays a key role in completing the entire process of communication.

Non-verbal communication as you can correctly assume is communication without words. You communicate non-verbally through your eyes, gestures, facial expressions, touch, odour, body posture, and space usage, what you wear and when someone receives these signals and more importantly understands them. Every non-verbal communication is society specific and universal specific (thanks to the power of media). Without deciphering or understanding the non-verbal communication, the exercise is useless. One can say the same for verbal communication as to an Englishman speaking Chinese in London or an original Red Indian native trying to communicate with Columbus through the smoke signals.

Even if you remain silent and someone attributed meaning to your silence, communication has taken place. If, on the other hand, you gestured or smiled and no one perceived these movements, then no communication has taken place. This does not mean that both sender and receiver have to give the same meanings to the signals (the gestures, the smile). It merely means that for communication is complete when there is a sender and receiver of the message signals. Thus, a verbal and non-verbal message must communicate a specific meaning.

Non-verbal messages can communicate exact the same meanings as the verbal messages. Non-verbal signals serve the same purposes identified for communication in general as well. First, non-verbal messages help us to discover to learn, to acquire information about the world and about other people. Non-verbal messages like the smile, the eye contact, the leaning forward, and of course, the kiss helps to establish and maintain relationships. We signal that we like another person first through non-verbal signals followed by verbal messages. At the same time, of course, our non-verbal messages can destroy and dissolve interpersonal relationships. When you avoid eye contact, touching, frown more than smile, voice without warmth, nostrils flare or studied silence; these are non-verbal signals to distance yourself from the other person. You can use non-verbal messages to help. Gently touching an ill person's face, hugging someone who is in pain, or helping an old person walk are common examples. Non-verbal messages are a good tool to persuade others; for example, your posture and clothing communicate your self-confidence; your steady gaze communicates conviction that you are right; your facial expression communicates that the advertised product tastes good. Besides, non-verbal messages are also used to play, act and perform. Theatre performances, tickling or playing with a young child, making funny faces, and drawing pictures are simple examples.

Most of the non-verbal communication occurs in conjunction with verbal messages. They reinforce the verbal duel and intent and serve a meta-communication function. That is, non-verbal messages often comment on or communicate something about other messages. Non-verbal messages serve to emphasize some part of the verbal communication. For example, raising your voice to reinforce or lay stress on a particular word or phrase, banging your fist on the table to buttress your commitment, or gazing longingly into someone's eyes conveying, "I need you."

You use non-verbal communication to compliment, to nuance the issue not communicated by your verbal message. Thus, you may mimic laughter when telling a story (to suggest that you find it extremely humorous) or frown and shake your head when recounting someone's wrong doings (to suggest your tacit disapproval). You may also deliberately contradict your verbal messages with non-verbal movements, for example, by crossing your fingers or winking to indicate that you are lying.

Your body part movements regulate or control the flow of verbal messages, when you purse your lips, lean forward, or make hand gestures to indicate that you want to speak. You might also put up your hand or vocalise your pauses (for example, with "hm" or "ah") to indicate that you have not finished and are not ready to relinquish the floor to the next speaker. You can repeat or restate the verbal message non-verbally. You can, for example, follow your verbal "Is that fine?" with raised eyebrows and a questioning look or motion with your head or hand to repeat your verbal "Let's move."

Communication Statistics

Assumedly, what we speak as a colleague, or a student, or a teacher or a senior, the object is that the target audience should understand the message we want to put through. How indignant we become when we find things said or told are not adhered too. However, have we ever introspected on the quality of our communication? Most of us are largely pathetic non-communicators. We are unsure of what we want to convey. The studies conducted reveal the percentage of understanding gained from the spoken word. It is considerably less than the meaning that people gain from listening to a person's tone of voice and looking at their non-verbal communication.

The breakdown is as under:

Seven per cent of the spoken words constitute the whole gamut of communication. Thus, speech is a minuscule part of our lives and worth knowing but not turning your hair grey on it.

The listener grasps thirty-eight per cent of the spoken words through the components of paralanguage such as intonation, hesitation noises, gesture and facial expression. However as it is a pitch of a voice, it is non-verbal in context, as it does not constitute a speech. If you need to communicate verbally as a public speaker or have effective verbal command over the language, then mate, it is your bread and butter.

Fifty-five per cent of the communication is non-verbal in its entirety. Combined with paralanguage, verbal communication is as good as dead in terms of percentages. In addition, this is the mother of communication and better be everyone's major food.

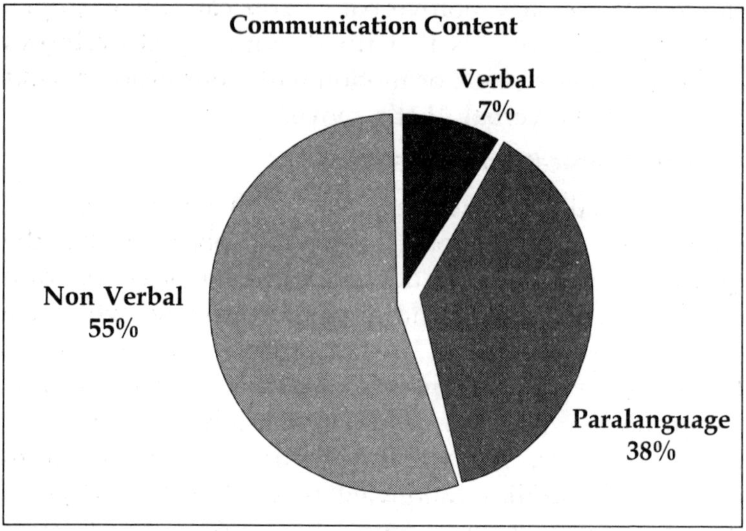

Now having given you a basic insight into what actually scientists and researchers constitute as communication let us proceed further and ask you a very simple question.

How do you code your communication?

Coding your communication is a very complex process. But remember that:

- The way you code your communication, the decoder will decode it the same way.
- As entire human body, the communication antenna, is involved in radiating communication energy, there is need to study the whole body in this aspect.

I am not a master on these issues. I hold no earth shaking educational degree to flout it on the issue. Nor I am any soft skilled trainer who has acumen of interacting with thousands of students. I only have my own knowledge, acquired, gleaned and deduced from my interactions in life. Given in subsequent narrations are the various codes (also known as channels) by which the humans communicate.

GENETIC COMMUNICATION

- Genes are the most conscientious communicators.
- They have the communication ability, which go back millions of years.
- They are the building blocks of life.
- They are also of the most conniving in nature.

Millions of years ago, a right set of atmospheric and ground conditions combined a few amino acids to fuse and create a living organism. Along with it came the genes, which would shape its survival on this planet. The genes adapt always to the environmental conditions, found a system in madness to survive by a continuous process of transformation. From each corner of the world, they muted, reformed to produce their ultimate creation, the human being along with hosts of other species. Even at this very moment, the genes are adapting to variation. They have connived with nature, time, our shortcomings, our cosmos and our future needs to remain on top of the evolution chain and importance. The skull of humans is expanding as facts yielded by million years old historical human skeletal finds come to surface. We are using our brains more. In another million years from now, if the human race exists, your skull may be the biggest part of your anatomy, and legs the shortest, as we no longer need them to walk to go to various places. Blame all of this to the conniving genes.

If we dwell upon the genetic pool of living species, we will find many a common gene with a shark, a man, a raccoon or any bird. Therefore, we know these great tiny microorganisms of life connived with forces of nature, assessing the degree of survivability of each genetic make up, again manipulating, unless they created what they did.

Genes communicate in various ways.

If they did not communicate, how would you explain the existence of the following?

- Aggression amongst entire living species when threatened
- Child crying on birth
- The act of suckle by two-hour-old born infants
- Tears in pain
- One-day-old born blind and deaf child, laughing like you and me
- Isolated aborigines stamping their feet in anger
- Family history of genetic disorders such as diabetes, leukemia, heart attacks etc.

We cannot learn these things; these come back from our stored knowledge of genetic past. Present spectacular insight into study of medical genetics has revealed the genes, which control anger or aggression. Fusion of science with genes to evolve more effectively is a barrier long broken. Will we see Einstein's son being a next generation Einstein. Not a mere conjecture of possibility, but definitely, a certainty of future.

Genes are the first blocks of humans, which communicate. The scientists have broken frontiers in research, have successfully isolated the genes of effective communication radiators, and pass them on to the next life. Nevertheless, we can take heart from the knowledge that unless the science of genetics turns on its head, in the next few years, genetic inconsistencies will marginally hamper the effective communication. Therefore, until that genetic wonder happens, we can only hope that our parents pass on good genes, so that we can live healthy and communicate effectively. Russian studies lead by the Russian biophysicist and molecular biologist Pjotr Garjajev into DNA sciences has shown the following interesting and revolutionary information:-

- Words and frequencies without cutting out and replacing single genes can influence and reprogram me the DNA.
- Protein building needs only 10 per cent of the DNA. The other 90 per cent considered "junk DNA" serves as data storage, communication, and the genetic code.
- Living DNA substance, in living tissue, will always react to language-modulated laser rays and even to radio waves by proper frequencies. This finally and scientifically explains why affirmations, hypnosis and the like can have such strong effects on humans and their bodies. It is entirely normal and natural for our DNA to react to language.
- DNA can cause disturbing patterns in a vacuum, thus producing magnetised wormholes! Wormholes are the microscopic equivalents of the so-called Einstein-Rosen bridges near black holes (left by burnt-out stars). These are the tunnel connections, which transmit

information outside of space and time. The DNA attracts these bits of information and passes them on to our consciousness. We in earth call this telepathy, hyperactive communication where information feed without studying for it is available to give or predict. I can only shout from top of my house wow and wow.

Therefore, now we can prove the old sciences we earlier frowned upon as not tested by the right spirit of scientific temper. It brings to fore the concept of faith healing, telepathy, group consciousness, aroma or magnet therapy, Feng Shui/Vastu Shastra, astronomy and anything that produces frequencies, which can affect our genes/DNA to the realms of scientific facts and study. Now we know scientifically that genes talk, can talk and do talk. Thus, genes are the first building blocks of life, which evolved due to communication and its profound influence.

Now, let us consider the act of mating, which results in conception of living species. So many factors are involved for correct conception. First, you have to find a right mating partner. It will not come without communication harmony. The bodies of both the partners must be in harmony to produce required healthy sperms and ova. Secondly, the act must take place. Thirdly, the sperms must travel inside in harmony of the complex environment to find the right ova so these ovulate perfectly. Lastly, the genes have to match in genetic compatibility. It is a very complex process but accomplished only by communication of genes and their ability to flourish in harmonised environment.

Now having seen the conception, a pure act of genes conniving at each stage with forces of nature to succeed, let us learn about the baby in the womb.

WOMB COMMUNICATION

Womb is the first place where living species learn. As they develop in their mothers' womb, they start the first step of applied learning. They communicate happiness, discomfort and hunger by making demand on the host body. I have already given you a brief insight into womb communication. Let me explain further.

We know the ancient story of Abhimanyu, the son of legendry archer Arjuna. In the heat of battle of Krukshetra, he entered the 'chakravhayu'. Chakravhayu was a complex battle formation of multiple layers of defense, destroyable only if you fought from its middle ground. The art of survival depended on your ability to escape from chakravhayu. His father, Arjuna, was a master of it. Abhimanyu had learnt the art of entering the chakravhayu, in the womb of his mother, when her husband Arjuna had narrated the tale of defeating this battle formation. However, at the crucial juncture when he was narrating how to come out of it, Arjuna's wife, Draupadi, slept and the child in the womb of her mother could not hear the escape plan. Abhimanyu fought bravely after entering the chakravhayu and died fighting trapped inside it.

On the more realistic front let me narrate a personal story. I was a fan of singer Don Williams before marriage and my wife discovered the love for that precise music later. When she was carrying our first child, the tape recorder would endlessly play Don Williams music, right until her delivery. To our amazement, we found out that whenever we played Don Williams music, our elder son would suddenly become calm-quite from his cranky worst and smile and giggle afterwards. The two tales, one ancient and second very personal, highlight the fact that a child learns when it is still in the foetus form.

Your grandma would not have been far wrong, when she would ridicule and drill the younger mothers of her clan to read Mahabharata or Ramayana, during their pregnancy periods. They were unknowingly passing down the known wisdom of old.

- In the womb child receives his first inward communication.
- The mother has to be in mental, spiritual and physical communication harmony with the nature for the baby to develop correctly.
- Moreover, communication shapes your basic personality.

Scientists have now started discovering this acute phenomenon and state that the child behaves the way he behaves, until first two years of his life in what he acquires in the womb. Then other acquired cognitive experiences take over to mould the child's personality. The womb acquired knowledge manifests in the child until the age of two years when the child first time unlearns what he had learned in his mother's womb as forces of reality (real world experiences) overtakes his communication experience. The child goes through a 'cognitive disconnect' at that stage.

The most important issue with us is that knowing about it, what do we do.

- We establish the first contact with the child in womb.
- Establishing the first contact is the most difficult aspect of any communication.
- The first contact shapes how you will perceive things in future as an individual and as a judge on others.

Imagine the implication of wrong or botched up first contact, with your new boss, a new friend, newly married wife, two friendly but heavily armed patrols meeting in middle of a dense jungle or a surrendering enemy. The botched up first contact may label you rude, uncaring and unprofessional throughout your life and in the worst military scenario lose your life. It will take a Herculean effort to undo what you did wrong the first time.

Importance of the first contact is most paramount in hearing how will you communicate in future as an adult.

We as parents establish the first contact with our child. The first contact and subsequent contacts, with the new nurturing life have to be simple for the child in the womb to understand.

Imagine a child, who is listening, understanding and growing in the womb listening to the dose of daily fights, verbal and physical abuses, unhealthy diet, fearful atmosphere and unending unhappiness. What will be the future of the child in the real world when he had a very bleak life in the womb? Guesses are for the readers to make. I am not suggesting that the child cannot overcome the prenatal deficiencies but his life begins on a negative note. Do you want your child to start his life on a negative note? No sane parent would say yes. We as parents need to provide a continuous harmonious communication, which helps the child to develop into a good human being. Whether he is a happy, smiling, suspicious or a scowling child; all depends upon you.

The womb communication shapes the personality of the child. Latest studies on Fetal Senses reveal following:

- Babies in the womb are prepared to send and receive communication without benefit of the words, syllables, and phrases.
- Self-initiated and reactive movements, which precisely express needs, interests, and feelings, punctuate the daily experiences of communication, which mode of communication continues not only in uterus but after the birth too, throughout the life span. It is a universal human language.

- Based on the early development of the senses in the womb, a foetus remains in constant dialogue with the surrounding environment.
- Baby-body-talk includes various senses: responding to tastes and odours by abrupt behaviour changes reflecting pleasure or displeasure; reacting against strong light, noise, pressure, or pain by gestures of defense or escape; and reacting to different types of music by either wild kicking or by calming down to listen or rest. We should not argue with baby body language. Wow, I know for sure that this is very true.
- Ultrasound observations of behaviour in the womb reveal that foetuses show strong emotion. Amniocentesis of 16–20 weeks old foetus revealed fearful reactions including extreme fluctuations in heart rate and withdrawal from normal activity for a period of hours or even days. With increasing use of amniocentesis, women and doctors have witnessed aggressive actions toward the needle itself as babies attack the needle barrel from the side.
- The ability to signal distress by crying is a familiar aspect of infant behaviour. Cries can be compelling. Babies need no lessons in crying; adults, of course, need lessons in interpreting this crying. Measurements have shown that cries contain much information about disease, malnutrition, and genetic defects. Babies are sensitive to each other's cries and discriminate between animal, human, and electronic cry sounds. They respond most strongly to cries of babies their age. The emotional turmoil, which provokes crying already, exists in the womb and is audible if air reaches the area around the foetal larynx. The crying of the child in the uterus before birth is termed *Vagitus uterinus* - well documented in the ancient and modern medical literature.

- In the case of twins ultrasound studies reveal that they have uncovered body language including holding hands, kissing, playing, kicking and hitting each other. This communication before birth remains unpredicted in psychology.
- At birth, body talk is eloquent whether asserting anger and rage with clenched fists or in relaxed gestures and even smiles, conveying pleasure. Newborns clearly communicate their feelings about what is happening to them by contortions of the face, writhing movements of the torso, flailing movements of arms and legs, by changing colour to angry red, dangerous blue or paleness, or by reassuring coos and gurgles. These obvious skills of communication flow from impressive skills of perception during both pre and postnatal existence.
- Babies begin learning language in the womb. An early discovery using acoustic spectrographs revealed that the first cry of a 900-gram baby already contained intonations, rhythms, and other speech features that matched with the mother's voice spectrograph. This proved that by about 26 weeks of gestation, this baby had already acquired certain features of its "mother tongue."
- Studies that are more recent reveal unexpected learning of story passages and child rhymes in uterus, a precocious demonstration of early language perception and learning. After birth, babies show more interest in listening to an adult speaking in the mother tongue rather than in a different language. Language studies have demonstrated that babies perceive the smallest units of sound, the phonemes, even better than adults do for about the first year of life. Superior lip-reading skills manifest when babies quickly detect which sound track matches the talking faces they are watching. They also quickly select the appropriate

emotional sound track for the faces they are watching. In addition to these lip-reading skills, both premature and full-term babies read faces so well that they can immediately imitate a wide-open mouth, a protruding tongue, or mimic expressions of happiness, sadness, or surprise – superb communication skills.

- Newborns arrive in this world equipped with universal human languages made possible by the voluntary movement which begins around ten week's gestational age. Early expressive movement is facilitated by a spectrum of developing senses including at least touch, thermal experiences, taste, odour, hearing, licking, sucking, and even vision. The communication repertoire includes verbal and non-verbal expressions, body colour, emotional behaviours, crying, withdrawal, and hand gestures, a range of facial statements, instant imitation, and lip-reading. Thus, all humans are prepared to send and receive messages and talk to parents long before the development of formal language.

VERBAL COMMUNICATION

Words are the basic tool of communication and not a substitute for action.

The word formation happens from sound. The first thing a baby does when it emerges out of his mother's womb is to make sound. The last thing you do when you faint or die is to stop making sound. However, making sound is a very funny business.

Man kept on uttering sound in isolation first, the tribal groups later. It took him a very long time to interpret right sounds with same audibility characteristic to know its universal meaning. It was as simple as that. Once the humans could utter or make a repeated sound and give it an identifiable written word, the era of language was born. Given the language, the power of expression was born which could record previous knowledge, build upon the acquired knowledge and offer reasoning to develop more.

Once a universal meaning within a group of humans was established, they slowly converted it into a language of masses for that particular area. However, due to the geographical isolation of humans interpreted these sounds differently in various regions, which led to the growth of various languages.

The scientists have found a direct link between the initial growths of intelligent cultures to the level of phonetic development in the cultures. The tribes, which had few phonetic sounds developed less than those who had more. In English, we have 26 sound letters, while in Hindi 53, little more in Sanskrit and thousands in Chinese. Was that the reason that all early scientific developments took place in China or India or around those regions where the language matured to reasoning, like in Greece and Rome? Red Indians of Australian original natives, despite uninterrupted period of thousands of years of free development lived in tented clusters and little material development. Europe lived in dark ages until renaissance and education tempered by scientific quest gave it the unique power to rule the world. The peculiarities of sound are:

- However, making sound does not get you always understood. It only makes you announce your presence only to those not looking your way.
- However, making sound does not get you always heard. It only makes you lonelier, especially when the people looking your way do not register what you say.
- However, making sound is the first step to communication linked to evolution of the humankind to present technological marvels.

Thus, sound or verbal communication has history of society's development attached to it. Verbal communication communicates your culture and power of reasoning. Sound enables you to command men, teach and preach, sing; communicate across the oceans and stars, allay fears, tell stories; pray, grunt in love, cry in pain and so on.

Verbal communication conveys and cements personnel relationships.

That relationship withers or dies, which has more bouts of silence than soothing sounds, has more bouts of monotonous sounds than the bouts of silence. That relationship flourishes where the sounds are harmonised, soothing and continuous despite minor blips of harshness or silence.

Sound is the most troublesome condition to remove from your thoughts.

The sound is so encompassing that it surrounds, is soaked, and permeates into every aspect of your body, mind and soul. Ask great sages how to learn to focus or meditate to bring calmness to your agitated mind. Everyone starts with a teaching plan that centres on how to eliminate sound. I challenge you to eliminate sound from your surroundings right now. It is not possible to eliminate sound unless you orient yourself and such an orientation is a time-consuming process. Eliminating sound from mind brings peace, tranquility and spirituality.

Sound is the external stimulus, which affects each gene of your body. Sound has a profound impact on a human body. If you succeed in the elimination of sound from your body, it assumes mental or spiritual connotations. You can sense it coming, hit you and rebound.

There are certain parameters, which hold true for verbal communication. Its impact is everlasting. It shapes your physical and emotional response, which can be immediate, retrospective, or prospective. Its impact is soothing, harsh, depending upon what you want to convey in that it conveys many meanings, direct, indirect, and subtle – depending upon the intelligence of the sender. What you hear and understand depend upon the intelligence and attentiveness of the receiver. You can train to improve what sounds you make to make your communication delivery more effective.

Silence has its own connotations in communications.

Silence is also one of the most powerful medium of verbal communication, not fully appreciated in the vocal madness of sounds. It commands more respect and meaning than vocal communication and is others' alter ego. Like words and gestures, silence too communicates important meanings and serves important functions. The golden advantages of silence are as follows:

- Silence allows the speaker time to think, time to formulate and organize his or her verbal communications. Before messages of intense conflict, as well as before those confessing undying love, there is often silence. Again, silence seems to prepare the receiver for the importance of these future messages.
- Some people use silence as a weapon to hurt others. We often speak of giving someone "the silent treatment." After a conflict, for example, one or both individuals may remain silent as a kind of punishment. Silence used to hurt others may also take the form of refusing to acknowledge the presence of another person, as in disconfirmation here silence is a dramatic demonstration of the total indifference one person feels toward the other.
- Sometimes silence is a response to personal anxiety, shyness, or threats. You may feel anxious or shy among new people and prefer to remain silent. By remaining silent, you preclude the chance of rejection. Only when you break your silence and attempt to communicate with another person, you risk rejection.
- Silence is an effective mean to prevent communication of certain messages. In conflict situations, silence yields the best of results in preventing certain topics from surfacing restraining thereby both the parties from saying things they may later regret. In such situations,

silence often allows us time to chill out before expressing hatred, severe criticism, or personal attacks, which are irredeemable.

- Like the eyes, face, and hands, silence serves in communicating emotional responses. Sometimes silence communicates a determination to be non-cooperative or defiant, by refusing to engage in verbal communication; you defy the authority or the legitimacy of the other person's position.
- Silence is often useful in communicating annoyance, particularly when accompanied by a pout. I am able to resist temptations, when displaying I know expression, arms crossed in front of the chest, there is work to be done and nostrils flared. Silence may express affection or keep working at a difficult, uninteresting task, love, especially when coupled with long and longing stares into each other's eyes.

Paralanguage shows another important aspect to communication.

Paralanguage is the vocal but non-verbal dimension of speech and is more important than the vocal language. It has to do not with what you say but with how you say it. In addition to the tone, stress, pitch, highness or lowness, paralanguage includes such voice qualities as rate of speed, volume or the loudness, rhythm of the speech and lastly the vocalisations you make in crying, whispering, moaning, belching, yawning, and yelling. Variation in any of these features communicates a different meaning. When you speak quickly, for example, you communicate something different from when you speak slowly. Even though the words may be the same, if the speed (or volume, rhythm, or pitch) differs, the meanings people receive will also differ. As I am not a linguist or a language/speech impact specialist, but still I do no justice to the subject that amplifies both the side of the communication modes, verbal and non-verbal aspects. This aspect does affect the confidence of a speaker, impact of verbal message on the target audience, amplification of your non-verbal content of delivery of message. Beside it is all about or the reflections of your personality as you want it to react to/with the environment.

I will not dwell on other aspects of psychology and other intricate vocal innuendos or its direct opposite of silence, which complete this mode of communication. It is completely a separate study in itself and is beyond the scope of this book wherein I have touched only on aspects, which affect us.

In army for us, this mode or channel of communication is the key element in commanding men. There is an old cliché that "with words you govern men", and I have immense faith in it. Voice instills calm, urgency, faith, raise morale, inspire men, make thousand men charge at the enemy regardless to loss of their lives, provide sympathy, command, fear, authority, punishment, care and all those seemingly unfathomable factors which make soldiers behave the way they do. I have seen that soldiers will do anything if the voice is true, touches their heart and they respect it.

POSTURE COMMUNICATION

"The body says what words cannot."

—Martha Graham

Two areas of the body are especially important in communicating messages. First, the movements you make with your body communicate; second, the general appearance of your body communicates.

Researchers in kinesics or the study of non-verbal communication through face and body movements identify five major types of movements; emblems, illustrators, affect displays, regulators, and adaptors as follows:

- **Emblems** are a body gesture that directly translate into words or phrases for example, the OK sign, the thumbs-up for "good job," and the V for victory. You use these consciously and purposely to communicate the same meaning as the words. However, emblems are culture specific, so be careful when using your culture's emblems in other cultures. Waving hand sideways is a welcome sign in America, a no sign in Germany and offensive gesture in Greece.
- **Illustrators** enhance the verbal messages they accompany. For example, when referring to something to the left, you might gesture toward the left. Most often, you illustrate with your hands, but you can also illustrate with head and general body movements. You might use illustrators to communicate the shape or size of objects you are talking.
- **Affect displays** are movements of the face (smiling or frowning, for example) but also of the hands and general body (body tension or relaxation, for example) that communicate emotional meaning. Affect displays are often unconscious. You smile or frown unknowingly. At other times, however, you may smile

consciously, trying to convey your pleasure or satisfaction.

- **Regulators** are behaviours that monitor, control, coordinate, or maintain the speaking of another individual. When you nod your head, for example, you tell the speaker to keep on speaking; when you lean forward and open your mouth; you tell the speaker that you would like to say something.
- **Adaptors** are gestures that satisfy some personal need, such as scratching to relieve an itch or moving your hair out of your eyes. Self-adaptors are self-touching movements such as sucking your thumb or scratching your eyebrows. Alter-adaptors are movements directed at the person with whom you are speaking, such as straightening someone's ruffled hair or straightening a person's tie or folding your arms in front of you to keep others at a comfortable distance from you. Object-adaptors are gestures focused on objects, such as smiling over or shredding an examination questionnaire.

As already narrated, the human body is an antenna for radiation and in its skeletal state is the biggest visible one. The posture captures your eye the first and generates its own implications.

Posture communication is also an extension of limb communication. They both complement each other but are different from each other. While the limb communication displays the emotional state of an individual, the posture communication generally reflects the physical state of the individual. When you lean forward to speak or lean against a wall with a smile on your lips, it is a signal of your deep affection you harbour for other person. A few examples are: a person standing erect or slouching, sitting or sleeping, fidgety or calm; athletic, medium built, bulky or obese; running, jogging or walking.

Posture communication plays a very important role in defence services. The military bearing is an apt example to pick a soldier amongst the group of civilians. The way an officer gives orders, the way he stands, the way he moves, the way he handles his weapon; all these convey to the soldier the determination of the officers intent to complete the mission.

Posture communication has also taken many a varied form and meaning. From looking cool, from aping the idols, from looking military, from representing the attitude set of a group, from symbolic manifestation, organised violence or non-violence, and representing your personal attitude or representing that of a group.

Posture communication has also many peculiarities. It provides the first contact perceived input through eye communication between the two parties generally followed by gesture or vocal communication. The impression of posture communication is long lasting; it can be for an individual or a group; it displays generally the physical state of the individual; and amplifies individual or group attitude.

LIMB COMMUNICATION

"I do not try to dance better than anyone else. I only try to dance better than myself."

—***Michail Baryshnikov***

The limbs, the arms and legs, speak a very special language. It is non-verbal in nature but as powerful as any verbal duel. This lingua franca of the limbs varies from culture to culture and continent to continent. However, the wonder of modern day technology, of shrinking the world we live in, has also increased the visibility of this mode of communication. This mode of communication owes its origin to the way people interact. It is a part of the culture of any society. The geographical area and natural forces that sweep that area also temper it. However, some of its key components remain the same. Maybe the genetic communication shapes this product too.

- They attribute continuous leg shaking to nervousness or impatience for a man, while a woman crossing and uncrossing legs denotes that she is sexually stimulated.
- Standing arms akimbo, for a man, to power.
- A woman standing arms across her chest, to give a signal not to come closer and needs protection from big bad world.
- A man, crossing his hands across his genitals while sitting, signifies that he is having problems or is an unsure person.
- Embrace conveys warmth.
- A child clutching his mother from behind means that the child is seeking protection.

There are universal connotations and local too. One has to know them as a separate study.

The Limb Communication has the following peculiarities.

- It is seen, perceived and understood, to represent an individual.
- Its interpretation lays down ground rules for present communication.
- It conditions the further response.
- It generally highlights four major aspects of the individual.
  - **Passivity** of the subject.
  - **Emotional state** of the subject.
  - **Aggressiveness** of the subject.
  - **Physical state** of the subject.

• It may not always be true to your stereotyping.

It is the impression you want to convey as the individual.

GESTURE COMMUNICATION

This communication is further refinement of limb communication. Gesture communication is a communicatory movement, usually of head or hands, intended to convey an intent. A chain of private thought sometimes evokes it without the communicatory purpose but more often than not it is very specific.

A few examples could be *Namaste* or a handshake is the gesture of welcome; middle finger pointed upward is a derogatory gesture; a woman shaking her hips repeatedly is a provocative gesture of sexual connotation; Winston Churchill's famous 'V' was a gesture for victory during World War II. An army salute is a gesture of paying compliment in defence services; bow is a gesture of accepting other's importance; touching the feet of elders in Indian context is the mark of paying respect: a thumb pointed down for a Roman Emperor was a message to slay and in present context of things not looking good.

Gestures are also reflective of history and specific to particular societies. A same gesture may have a different meaning to another race or community.

Gesture as a full fledged language is for the conveyance of ideas and to effectively communicate, to or by, deaf mutes, by use of specific gestures. Gestures are also ingrained in your brain. You know what they mean and that gesture will elicit a particular response. An example is given below in the illustration.

Gestures in military serve to retain surprise eliminate noise, save time etc. Armies across the world use gestures,

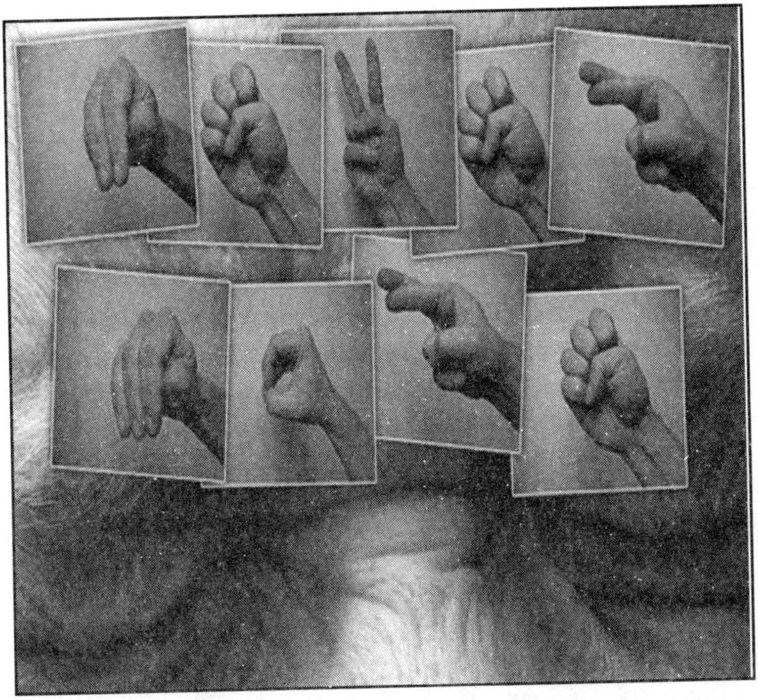

which gestures vary from army to army. The gestures are precise with very specific meanings and have no ambiguity; for example, to establish a firebase or ambush the enemy just one gesture will suffice for a number of interdependent communications.

From the above, the dichotomy of gestures into two categories is obvious, namely, *(a)* social gestures and *(b)* specific gestures. Nonetheless, all the gestures have a specific meaning. Socially accepted gestures become a part of our memory because of their acceptance in the society. We have learnt these gestures through the medium of friends, books, magazine and other forms of electronic media. As for specific gestures for deaf or the military, professionals on the subject teach these gestures in the classrooms. The distinct features of the gestures are that they refine the content of limb and posture communication; throw out a specific intent; that besides, gestures are non-emotional representation of emotions and desires. Furthermore, gestures save time, as the implied verbal communication is already broken down to the ultimate action to complement the verbal communication.

Gestures initiate action, without verbal command.

Gestures are steeped in history.

The famous middle finger gesture came about when before the Battle of Agincourt in 1415, the French, anticipating victory over the English, proposed to cut off the middle finger of all captured English soldiers. Without the middle finger it would be impossible to draw the renowned English longbow and therefore they would not be able to fight in the future. To the bewilderment of the French, the English won a major upset and mocked at the defeated French by waving their middle fingers.

How I wish we had never invented talking language. Nagging was much easier in sign language. When you can kick and punch then why talk and shout?

FACIAL COMMUNICATION

The face of the individual conveys facial communication. This form of communication is visible from the combination of contractions and expansions of the muscles in the face. These muscles contract and expand to the external (touch, heat) or the internal (mind state) stimulus. They are the second nearest set of communicators to the brain. Hence, reaction to any stimulus is almost instantaneous. It is due to this sudden response that this forms a very important study in itself in interrogation techniques. A few examples of facial communication are laughter, crying, spontaneous rising of eyebrows, sticking out tongue, flared nostrils etc. Facial communication represents happiness, hate, scorn; fear, pain, anger; excitement, acceptance and genuineness.

Facial communication amplifies reactions to external or internal stimulus. Every human being reacts to a situation differently depending upon his\her perception of the situation. Genetic communication conditions the reactions. However, depending on the constitution of individual, reactions happen in varying degrees of force. Let me explain this as follows:

- Two people can be angry or very angry but the shades of anger as reflected by the colour or the contraction of the facial muscles will be entirely different. Similarly, not all happy people laugh with same gusto or children with same degree of physical hurt cry in similar tenor.
- Anger can only be represented as anger in each individuals face, but to the perceiver, the angry contracted muscles of anger may enable you to burst you in a bout of lunatic laughter, as it may seem to be comic to you.
- In a given dangerous situation, one may remain calm while the other may break into a sweat.
- Not all in a group laugh with same intensity to a joke. Some smile, some laugh mutedly, some laugh loudly, some guffaw and some guffaw clutching their stomachs. To the same stimulus, people react differently.

This form of communication can trace its origins imbibed through genetic and womb communication and it gathers its strength or weakness from them. Thus, facial communication also has its own unique peculiarities such as it varies in intensity from individual to individual; it radiates the first true unconditioned response or a reaction; the intensity of reaction is based on the perception and understanding of the perceiver; it displays emotions. However, professionals and actors can suppress or modify this communication code.

Throughout your interactions, your face communicates various messages, especially your emotions. Facial movements alone seem to communicate the degree of pleasantness, agreement, and sympathy felt; the rest of the body does not provide any additional information. The emotions of happiness, surprise, fear, anger, sadness, disgust, contempt, and interest are subjective though; the facial expressions of these emotions are primary affect displays: they indicate relatively pure, single emotions. Other emotional states and other facial displays are combinations of these various primary emotions known as affect blend. You communicate the blended feelings with different parts of your face. Thus, for example, you may experience both fear and disgust at the same time. Your eyes and eyelids may signal fear, and movements of your nose, cheek, and mouth area may signal disgust.

As you grow, you learn your culture's non-verbal system of communication. You also learn certain facial management techniques, for example, to hide certain emotions and let others show on your face. These are explained as follows:-

- **Intensifying** helps you to exaggerate a feeling; for example, to exaggerate your surprise when friends throw you a party, so as to make your friends feel better.

- **De-intensifying** helps you to underplay a feeling; for example, to cover up your own joy in the presence of a friend who didn't receive such good news.
- **Neutralising** helps you to hide feelings; for example, to cover up your sadness so as not to depress others.
- **Masking** helps you to replace or substitute the expression of one emotion for the emotion you're really feeling; for example, to express happiness in order to cover up your disappointment about not receiving the gift you had expected.

The facial feedback hypothesis holds that your facial expressions influence physiological arousal. One learns facial management techniques along with display rules, which tell you what emotions to express when; they are the rules of appropriateness. For example, when someone gets bad news in which you may secretly take pleasure, the display rule dictates that you frown and otherwise non-verbally signal your displeasure. If you violate this kind of display rule, others will consider you insensitive.

The accuracy with which people can encode and decode emotions through facial expressions remains the biggest problem. One problem confronting us as we try to answer this question is that it is difficult to separate the ability of the encoder from the ability of the decoder. Thus, a person may be quite adept at communicating emotions non-verbally, but the receiver may prove insensitive. On the other hand, the receiver may be good at deciphering emotions, but the sender may be inept. Research reveals that women are better than men are at both encoding and decoding non-verbal cues for the simple reason that women play roles that are more different in society. They have learned different adaptive techniques and skills to help them perform these roles from being friendlier, nurturing, and supportive and surviving the label of weak sex physically. Accuracy also varies with the emotions. Some emotions are easier to encode and decode than others.

Surprisingly Charles Darwin was the first to publish the first major scientific study of facial communication in 1872. He concluded that many expressions and their meanings are universal. He was one of the first to give some thought to the communication process - so what if it came in a round about way of studying apes and monkeys as a thesis to prove that they were your forefathers. See below a half-tone. Can you analyze the expression on her face? Is she laughing or crying? Is she happy or sad? Most importantly is her face communicating anything to you?

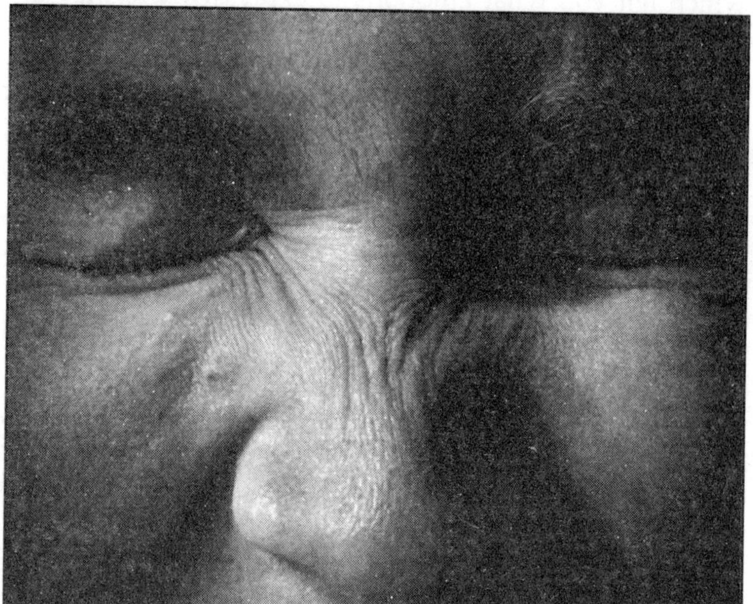

EYE COMMUNICATION

Eyes never lie.

Eyes have a language all of their own. They have a very subtle form of speaking that is hard to define, but you know it when you see eyes that "speak": they narrow, deepen, greet; adore, invite, suggest; implore, insist, caress; propose and promise. They also glow with knowledge, twinkle mischievously and set afire the sexual desire, without uttering a word.

Eye contact and facial expressions provide important social and emotional information; people, perhaps without consciously doing so, look into each other's eyes for positive or negative mood signs. In some contexts, the meeting of eyes arouses strong emotions. Eye contact is also an important element in flirting, where it may serve to establish and gauge the other's interest in some situations. A person's direction of gaze may indicate to others where his or her attention lies. Recent studies suggest that eye contact has a positive impact on the retention and recall of information and may promote learning that is more efficient. In adults, eye contact shows personal involvement and creates intimate bonds. Mutual gaze narrows the physical gap between humans. Eyes are the window to the brain and are the nearest external communicators to it. Despite being the smallest visible component of communication, they are the biggest receptors of communication. Besides, eyes are the fastest means of communication in grasping the situation; they enable to establish the first contact and shape your present and subsequent communications. The first way any two people connect is by looking into each other's eyes. Before the exchange of a single word, the eyes transmit a message of welcome or not being welcome. Eyes are always assessing, sizing and evaluating threats. When you look deep into eyes and eyes smile, you are telling your interest in the person.

You perceive the world as you see it.

In one glance, lasting not more than a microsecond, you can capture the canvass of an entire valley, complete wedding scene, a fair, a battle or a market place. It captures the moving canvass of anything, from heavens to stars, to hallucinations.

However, as true for other forms of communications, its actual capture of any communication depends upon the perception of the receiver. Two humans given the same landscape may see the same larger picture; say as of a war, but subtle hidden communications; say an enemy offering a hand of friendship in one corner of the earlier war canvass, may have different interpretations of both. One might say it is an offer of peace while the other may say it is sign of capitulation.

Thus, what you see and make out of it is based on your combined acumen of earlier such sightings, how it effects your daily life, your take on its history, your conviction about its goodness, how your family, peers or country perceive it and most importantly how you as an individual perceive it. A few important aspects of eye communication are that sight is always capturing data, is always comparing; it brings the burden of history, the burden of future in your communication, the burden of present dealing in your communication. Sight is the mirror of your brain. As an eye glimpses directly in your brain, it provides direct access to the thought interrupting with tremendous speed every second in your brain tempered adequately with the emotions of heart.

We all in our lives have seen, happy eyes, sad eyes, silly eyes, mischievous eyes, pain-filled eyes, love-filled eyes, loveless eyes, cold eyes, bitchy eyes, starving eyes, lying eyes, shifty eyes, trust worthy eyes, looks could kill eyes, sexy eyes, suggesting eyes, stopping eyes, positive eyes and negative eyes. The list could go on endlessly, but that is not the point. The point to make is that your eyes reflect the deep recesses of your brain. In simple words, your eyes reveal your inner state of mind.

If eyes lied so convincingly then it would not have been the case where interrogators, parents, teachers or anyone for that matter seeking truth would not stare in to your eyes when they will ask a question and nor would you look down if you were not replying in any sense negative or false.

Our anatomical eyes reveal us the physical aspect of communication. In realms of spirituality, we communicate with our third eye, just above the bridge of your nose. Do a simple exercise: close your physical eyes and tell your friend to point a finger at your third eye and get it near the skin randomly. Nine times out of ten, I can tell when the accusing finger is less than an inch away. That goes to prove that the location of the third eye does communicate and receive some vibrations. It is for us to concentrate and maximize that energy. Believe me all great sages have it. Build the capacity in you to see from your third eye. Its three most important aspects are:-

1. Eye communication gives the direct access to your brain.
2. Eye communication gives you the direct access to the state of your brain.
3. Eye communication gives you the direct access to the emotional turmoil your brain is trying to find recourse in.

The **study of oculesis**, that is the research on the messages communicated by the eyes shows that these messages vary depending on the duration, direction, and quality of the eye behaviour. This is explained as under :-

- The **average duration** of mutual gaze is about 2 seconds. When eye contact falls short of this amount, you may think the person is uninterested, shy, or preoccupied. When the appropriate amount of time is exceeded, you may perceive the person as showing unusually high interest.
- The **direction** of the eye also communicates different messages. The rule for the public speaker is to scan the entire audience, not focusing for too long on or ignoring any one area of the audience in particular. When you break these directional rules, you communicate different meanings abnormally high or

low interest, self-consciousness, nervousness over the interaction, and so on.

- The **quality** of eye behaviour; how wide or how narrow your eyes get during interaction, also communicates meaning, especially interest level and such emotions as surprise, fear, and disgust.

EYE CONTACT

Eye contact serves two main functions: one, to seek feedback; in talking with someone, we look at her or him intently, as if to say, "Well, what do you think?" In public speaking, you may scan hundreds of people to secure this feedback; two, to inform the other person that the channel of communication is open and that he or she should now speak. This is a routine feature vis-à-vis conversation.

See the smiling eyes below in the figure. Can she smile true if her eyes were not smiling?

Eye movements may also signal the nature of a relationship, whether positive attentive glance or negative eye avoidance. You can also signal your power through visual dominance behaviour. The average speaker, for example, maintains a high level of eye contact while listening and a lower level while speaking. When people want to signal dominance, they may reverse this pattern maintaining a high level of eye contact while talking but a much lower level while listening.

By making eye contact you psychologically, lessen the physical distance between yourself and another person. When you catch someone's eye at a party, for example, you become psychologically close though physically far apart.

Eye Avoidance

Eye avoidance has its own role to play. It fulfills the following tasks:

- When you avoid eye contact or avert your glance, you may help others maintain their privacy.
- Eye avoidance can also signal lack of interest in a person, a conversation, or some visual stimulus. At times, you may turn your eyes to block out unpleasant stimulus or you may listen to music with your eyes closed. Lovers often close their eyes while kissing, and many prefer to make love in a dark or dimly lit room.
- Pupil size also reveals your interest and level of emotional arousal. Your pupils enlarge when you are interested in something or when you are emotionally aroused.

Moreover, Eyes seldom lie.

TOUCH COMMUNICATION

Skin communicates: If it did not then you would not feel any sensation of, irritation, pain, hurt and caressing pats of love or the act of pleasure filled love making. This communication happens due to the sensory receptors in your dermis. The sent inputs are compared with historical inputs and thus interpreted. It has following important aspects:-

- **This communication draws on previous experience.** (You feel the goodness and softness of a fabric through comparison and previous reservoir of knowledge).
- **The body learns it automatically.** (Once burnt you will avoid the same situation at any cost).
- **It cannot be taught as it is experienced.** (Till the child does not burn his hand in fire, he will continue to play with fire, despite parental guidance. You only wear warm clothing in winter).
- **It is ever prevalent.** At any moment of time, in your conscious state, you can feel the heat, the clothes you are wearing, wind blowing across your face etc.
- It interacts with full surface area of your body, thus is **the largest communication receiver.**
- Touch also **displays many shades of emotions** for example, lovers, sexual touch, friendly touch, touch of encouragement (patting the back), informal touch (handshake) and offensive touch (bottom pinching in a crowded place) etc.
- Lastly touch signifies the level of comfortable closeness to an object or a person.

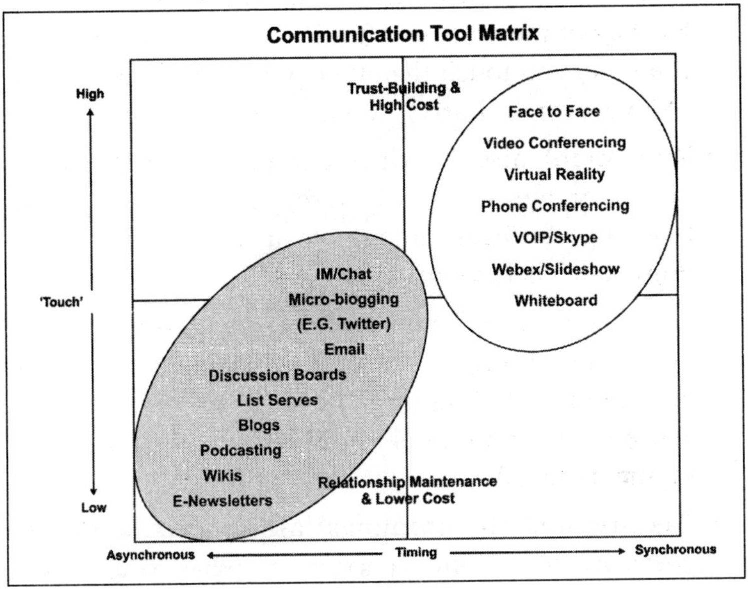

Touch communicates a wide variety of messages such as:

- Touch communicates positive feelings; for example, support appreciation, inclusion, sexual interest or intent, composure, immediacy, affection, trust, similarity and quality, and informality.
- Touch also stimulates self-disclosure and manifests in touch avoidance.
- Touch often communicates your intention to play, either affectionately or aggressively.
- Touch often communicates the status ladder of the society and the male hegemony. Pope, presidents, billionaires, important political leaders or people reserve the right to touch others and can do it at their free will. People at the lower rungs of society cannot touch people in high positions in society; a boss can barge at will in the office of his junior but the other way round is discourtesy.

- Touch may control the behaviours, attitudes, or feelings of the other person. To obtain compliance, for example, you touch the other person to communicate, "Move over," "hurry," "stay here," or "do it."
- You might also touch a person to, as if to say, "Look at me" or "look here." In some situations touching can even amount to a kind of non-verbal dominant behaviour.
- Ritualistic touching centers on greetings and departures; examples are shaking hands to say "hello" or "goodbye," hugging, kissing, or putting your arm around another's shoulder when greeting or saying farewell.
- Task-related touching is associated with the performance of some function, as when you remove a speck of dust from another person's coat, help someone out of a car, or check someone's forehead for fever.

However much you desire to touch, you also have the opposite preference not to touch a few objects - animate as also inanimate. Communication apprehension may be cause of touch avoidance. If you have a strong fear of oral communication, probably you have strong touch avoidance tendencies. Touch avoidance is also high in reticent persons. Both touch and self-disclosure are intimate forms of communication. People, who are reluctant to get close to another person by self-disclosing, seem reluctant to get close by touching. Noticeably, the old avoid touch with opposite sex more than the young do. As people get older, they touch less the members of the opposite sex; this decreased frequency of touching may lead them to avoid touching. Girls and women, children, touch each other more than the grown-ups do.

Touch is a very important communication in defence, especially in combat situations. A gentle touch by an officer or a sergeant will calm the new soldier's fears. A pat on shoulder is all a commanding officer needs to tell a work well done. It calms an agitated mind and instills confidence instantly.

The power of this communication has been exploited through invention of **brail language,** which has brought light and joy to millions of special people. It is their only mode of communication to learning, expressing their feelings, connecting to their gods and most importantly understanding this human nature which sets them apart.

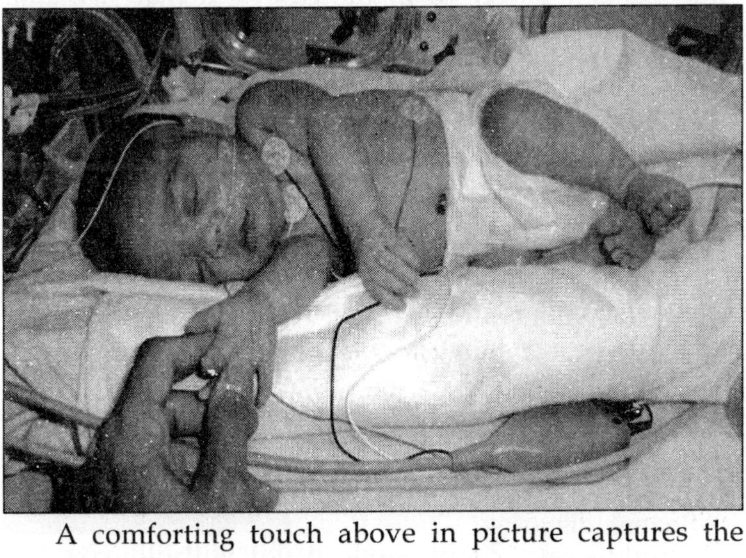

A comforting touch above in picture captures the essence and importance of this communication.

SPACE COMMUNICATION

Space communication is very subtle and affects all of us as we millions live in the restricted space around us. The space has its own ways of communicating its messages by subtle cues. Every human has his own comfort zone of space. We live in private comfort zone. We also live in social comfort zone. How we communicate with our body to other people in that space dictates what you want to convey.

You will embrace, kiss, hold hands, make love, stand next to and dance closely with only those persons who are your friends, emotional bonders and persons who you have immense faith. In any given group of persons, only a few share that comfort zone. With your other acquaintances, it translates into maintaining adequate body space. You are more controlled, mannered and aloof. In addition, this sort of communication signifies control, intention and power as in the case of a man standing next to the president; a toddler standing behind his mother; distance between the CEO's chair and yours; shaking hands of your idol. Besides, a teacher or a leader always stands on a platform vis-a-vis their audience.

Your use of space to communicate, an area of study known as proxemics, speaks loud and clear. Speakers who stand close to their listener, with their hands on the listener's shoulders and their eyes focused directly on those of the listener, communicate something very different from speakers who stand in a corner with arms folded and eyes downcast.

There are five proxemics distances:

- Spatial distance
- Intimate distance

- Personal distance
- Social distance
- Public distance

Spatial distance define the types of relationships between people and the types of communication they are likely to engage.

Intimate distance ranges from actual touching to 18 inches and the presence of the other individual is unmistakable.

Personal distance refers to the protective "bubble" that defines your personal space, ranging from 18 inches to 4 feet. This imaginary bubble keeps you protected and untouched by others.

Social distance, ranging from 4 - 12 feet, you lose the visual detail you have at personal distance. You conduct impersonal business and interact at a social gathering at this social distance. The more distance you maintain in your interactions, the more formal they appear. In offices of high officials, they arrange the desks in a manner that the official is certain of his distance from clients.

Public distance, from 12 to more than 25 feet, protects you. At this distance, you could take defensive action if threatened. On a public bus or train, for example, you might keep at least this distance from a drunken passenger.

Although at this distance you lose fine details of the face and eyes, you are still close enough to see what is happening.

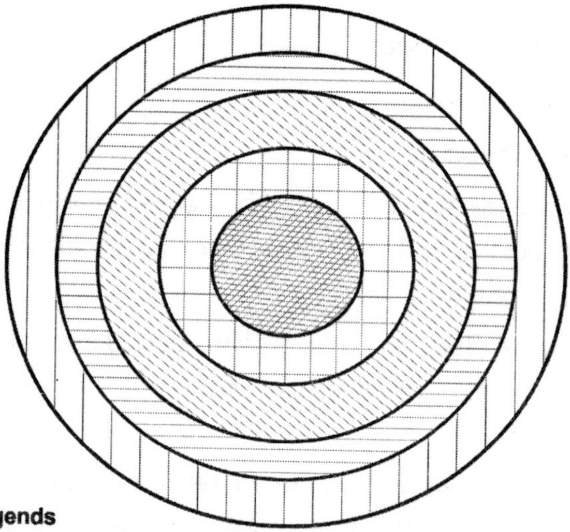

Legends

Public distance from 12 to more than 25 feet.

Social distance from 4-12 feet.

Personal distance from 18 inches to 4 feet.

Intimate distance from actual touching to 18 inches.

Intimate distance from actual touching to 18 inches.

Several factors influence space communication. Here are a few examples of how status, culture, subject matter, gender, and age influence space communication.

- People of equal status maintain less distance between themselves than the people of unequal status.
- When status is unequal, the higher-status person may approach the lower-status person more closely than the lower-status person would approach the higher-status person.
- Members of different cultures treat space differently. For example, people from northern European cultures

and many Americans stand fairly far apart when conversing; those from southern European and Middle Eastern cultures stand much closer.

- It is how people who interpret the close distances of others as pushy and overly intimate. It is equally easy to appreciate how those who normally stand close may interpret the far distances of others as cold and unfriendly.
- When discussing personal subjects you maintain shorter distances than with impersonal subjects.

The way you decorate your private spaces also communicates about you. The office with a mahogany desk and bookcases and oriental rugs communicates your importance and status within an organisation, just as a metal desk and bare floor indicate a worker much farther down in the hierarchy. Similarly, people will make inferences about you based on the way you decorate your home, by seeing the following:-

- The expensiveness of the furnishings may communicate your status and wealth; their coordination may convey your sense of style.
- The company of books you keep reflects your interests, and the arrangement of chairs around the 'idiot box' reveals how important watching television is to you. The contents of bookcases lining the walls reveal the importance of reading in your life.
- Computers, wide-screen televisions, well-equipped kitchens, and oil paintings of great grandparents, for example, all say something about the people who live in the home.
- Similarly, the absence of certain items will communicate something about you. Consider what messages you would get from a home where no television, phone, or books are visible.
- The way you decorate with infinite interest your particular room, shows what you place preference over in life for. It could be your living room or the

prayer room or the bar – this will definitely tell me that how much value you place in your personal life the spiritual life and of course the social life.

WRITING COMMUNICATION

"There was so much handwriting on the wall that even the wall fell down."

—***Christopher Morley***

The science of graphics or graphology is an accurate method in judging what people want to communicate. This mode is most interesting, as you have imbibed it since your childhood, from parents and teachers. Despite known and uniform modes of teaching mediums, no two humans have the similar handwriting. It is the direct outcome of your gained and embedded experiences learnt from the environment.

Take a blank piece of paper. It represents the environment and let ten people write on it a same paragraph. Some start the writing from top, others from middle. Some keep the left margin while others do not. Some scribble fast, others write very slowly. All have various angles of word slants; some write in neat parallel rows while others do not. Some do not overwrite while others strike through word after word; and, all have their peculiar loops and cuts.

What does it show?

Every human has his own peculiar characteristics to interact with environment, through this medium of writing as narrated under.

- **It reflects how an individual wants to communicate with the environment.** (How do you communicate with yourself with respect to past, present and future? It also tells how you adjust to a team and other people).
- **It reflects his basic character**. (He is open, stingy, artistic, dependable, honest, emotional, suicidal etc).

- **It reflects your physical energy levels**. (How energetic you are to your physical needs, exercise, lethargy, sexual satisfaction etc).
- **It is a direct peep into his mind**. (How dependent or independent you are in executing your tasks and work or the level of creativity you exhibit. It also lays down your personal rules of behaviour, your likes and dislikes, aversion, happiness, contentment with life).

Analysts have used this precise science to interpret human psychology and behaviour. All the employing organizations use handwriting analysis to interpret the personality of an individual. Criminologists use it for psychological profiling of criminals. Handwritings shape and actually reflect your mood swings, which in turn reveal your personality traits. With the increasing crime rate and the sophisticated tools used by criminals, handwriting analysis has become an independent subject.

The studies have proved that people with slanting and dropping letter d or b are emotionally unstable or the ones who use 'talon claws' under the letters g or y or q are very vindictive. The subject is vast and interesting and an avid communicator and boss must have working knowledge of it.

MIND COMMUNICATION

"The best and most beautiful things in the world cannot be seen or touched ... but are felt in the heart".

—Helen Keller

As mentioned earlier, telepathy is the truest form of communication. The required work is complete before the demand generates. It is what we call telepathy. Moreover, it happens amongst gods, sages, seers and godly men. How wrong can we be? Telepathy has been happening for millions of years among living species that inhabit this earth. Here are two prime examples.

- As an example from nature, when a queen ant separates from her colony, the remaining worker ants continue to building fervently according to plan. However, if the queen dies, all work in the colony stops. No ant knows what to do. Apparently, the queen transmits the "building plans" even if far away via the group consciousness with her subjects. She can be as far away as she wants, as long as she is alive.

- In humans, we come across hyper-communication when one suddenly gains access to information that is outside one's knowledge base. Such hyper-communication is either inspirational or intuitional (also in trance channelling). The Italian composer Giuseppe Tartini, for instance, dreamt one night that a devil sat at his bedside playing the violin. The next morning Tartini was able to note down the piece exactly from memory. He called it the Devil's Trill Sonata.

As regards telepathy, I have experienced it personally. I could establish telepathy with my wife twice and both times connected with her mundane needs, once for food and second time for need of money. Some people also have premonitions, foresee situations, have visions of future and weave a future tale. Some have been outright wrong, some vague, some just there and some accurate.

I think telepathy is the result of acute power of deduction, acquired through deep study of logic, having immense self belief in ones ability, foresee a problem, being proactive without self projection, having clarity of vision and thought, having insight of sequential forecasting and most importantly understanding human behaviour. Endowment of the supra attributes is possible for an angel of God – not for us frail humans.

Mind is the central processing unit of communication which unit receives messages, decodes, interprets and relays them. Mind communication has following idiosyncrasies as under.

- It occurs amongst people who are highly self-actualised.
- Thoughts neuro-impulses propagate it.
- It is immeasurable.
- It causes no friction.
- This communication makes no demand for compliance is willing.
- There are no known barriers to this form of communication.
- Humans rarely exhibit it while it is abundant in other living species.

Do you want the regular one or fat free lady?

STELLAR COMMUNICATION

In this age of science, it is difficult to make any practical scientist or a man agree to the fact that stellar bodies, communicate with human. They do, with their very own brand of communication. Stars communicate by light they emit, they communicate with radiations they throw out, they communicate with forces of gravity they exert on us and they have a special relationship with each individual they interact. Were it not so, one of the oldest sciences of mumbo-jumbo horoscopes would not have survived the falsehood for so long. There has to be some truth in it for it has captured the imagination of people for such long time. My logic is very simple. If moon affects the earth, and the ocean tides, then it affects the human body too.

I have my own take on the subject.

I am a firm believer in the occult influence of one stellar body on me – earth and moon.

Since my first month of the birth until age nine, every full moon, I would suffer from bronchial asthma with body temperature hovering between 103 and 104 degree. Many a learned doctor came, observed and went. They had never come across such a case of asthmatic bronchitis at Christian Medical College, Ludhiana. I suffered every month and when my senses became acute and as I grew older, I could comprehend the agony of my monthly torture. I cursed moon. Thankfully, this wolfish lunacy died on my attaining puberty but it left an indelible mark in my faith in the effects of heavenly bodies on our human bodies.

However, nowadays, I take recluse in the marvel of unfolding new frontiers of breakthrough technology, and it gives me pleasure to know that scientists are waking up to the fact of many issues such as telepathy, group consciousness, faith healing etc backed up by scientific studies and facts.

Genetic studies have revealed that by frequency, radiation, gravity influence the genes; hence, when genes make our whole body, they have a profound psychosomatic influence on us. I will not dwell any more on the planetary occult influence. I am convinced of the planetary influence on human mind and body. These impart certain characteristics, which are there for any observer to notice.

As per my observations, stellar communication **shapes your basic behaviour.**

The cartoon above relates to many things we have just talked about. So I feel is an apt summation.

SUMMATION

I have narrated in a very short form and independently are subjects so vast in content that each subject can form the basis of an independent study in itself. Study on these aspects is already in very advanced stages of discovery and knowledge generation. My own effort was to refocus on these issues once again. Again, there are many more communication codes such as smell, colour, clothing, which I have not dwelt. They also mean a lot to the public at large and armies in particular. The odour gives you perception of so many things and to us in uniform a situation to differentiate from life and death. (Mine detector dogs, smelling explosives, smell of enemy in an ambush, etc)

To sum up we have seen that human body has complex mechanisms to receive and radiate communication; we do positive actions provided we have decoded the sent communication perfectly; that complete communication is the manifestation of body (genes, limbs, gestures, face, touch and space), sight, speech, writing, mind and stars. They intervene and interact with each other so precisely to produce a perfect communicating medium; that silence is also a potent medium of communication.

We studied briefly the tonal content of speech, which amplifies all aspects of communication, and that speech per se is a very small effort in the whole process of communication.

God has blessed us with all communication skills. However, in some humans particular codes are more developed than the others. In some cases, men or women after having analysed their shortcomings in communication have trained themselves to overcome the difficulties. All is possible provided we have the will to do it. It is in us to find that what our own best mode of communication is. For that, first you have to find out by which mode inhibits you the maximum so that you can maximise it with adequate training. So let us study the aspects, which reduce your communication ability.

Internal Exploration

- Identify the communication codes in which you excel and those where you lag behind.
- Identify people around you who possess the best communication code as just learnt. (One person per each code)
- Study each individual with those great communication skills and adjudge where you fit in vis-à-vis that individual.
- Make your own communication strategy based on what you feel is best for you.

If you want to signal power non-verbally, try these suggestions:

- Walk slowly and deliberately. To appear hurried is to appear powerless, as if you were rushing to meet the expectations of those who have power over you. Use facial expressions and appropriate gestures to help you express your concern for the other person and the interaction and help you communicate your comfort and control of the situation.
- Consider standing relatively close to your listeners (even in public speaking); it will create proximity, likely to be more persuasive.
- Other things being equal, dress conservatively to influence others; conservative mode of dressing is associated with power and status.
- Select chairs you can get in and out of easily; avoid deep plush chairs that you will sink into and have trouble rising up.
- To communicate dominance with your handshake, exert more pressure than usual and hold the grip a bit longer than normal.
- Use consistent packaging; be careful that your verbal and non-verbal messages do not contradict each other, a signal of uncertainty and a lack of conviction.
- Be sure to respond in kind to another's eyebrow flash (raising the eyebrow as a way of acknowledging another person).
- When you break eye contact, direct your gaze downward; otherwise, you will communicate a lack of interest in the other person.

Chapter - 4

Communication Conflicts

"Generally speaking, the first non-violent act is not fasting, but dialogue. The other side, the adversary, is recognized as a person; he is taken out of his anonymity and exists in his own right, for what he really is, a person. To engage someone in dialogue is to recognize him, have faith in him. At every step in the non-violent struggle, at every level we try tirelessly to establish a dialogue, or re-establish it if it has broken down. When I say 'the other side,' that could be a group of persons or a government"

—H Goos-Mayr

In the act of leading daily life or simply living, each individual goes through the continuous catharsis of conflicts or finds him trapped in one. It is not a strange phenomenon but a natural way of things, so do not loose your hair on it. However, do lose your sleep on it, if you do not know how to handle this appendage to your existence as a human being. The manifestations and meanings can be many of these conflicts, but the process of conflict is constant regardless of your age. The conflict starts as early as you are born of having to make choices of learning, desiring, wanting what is denied, seeking comfort, being belly satiated etc. The issues compound as one grows up, increases interaction with society. Emotional body state of all humans is always seeking stability. If you have one, then you are a kin or the God itself. History is replete with examples of sages wandering, pondering until they achieved that stability in thought. This engenders two questions: one, why are the people in the continuous state of emotional and physical disharmony? Two, how have the emotionally stable people achieved this, so much sought after desired state, which we also refer to as "Nirvana"? Communication gap happens due to following:

- People remain in perpetual disharmony due to many reasons, which could be mismatch of their desires and wants;
- Inability to interpret what other wants.
- Inability to express what they want.
- Maybe certain personal deficiencies.
- The communication medium employed.
- The communication barriers encountered.
- The ability of your antennae being polished i.e. how powerfully you receive communication and emit communication.

If one goes through the reasons quoted above, the most startling deficiency, which comes to fore, is their inability to communicate with the environment they live in. Thus, discontentment and disharmony, though in part are psychological but largely correct communication abilities are responsible for these.

Emotionally stable people, have a unique way of simplifying their self-projections. They make no demands on the environment, thus they are in harmony with it. In other words, they have actuated their communication skills to a point, wherein they feel in harmony with the environment, always and every time.

When you have very few demands, you always connect the best with others. I think this trait is common to all the great sages and peers over the ages. However, here it would be incorrect to assume that only harmonized people are sages. There are people, who get good work done, are good leaders, are hard taskmasters, but they have one trait in them that they think through their communication process to every minute detail as to provide correct environment to others to work in. It can be a great mom or dad, or teacher, or any professional.

So if we look at people of both ends of spectrum are available those harmonised (a very select few) and those not harmonised.

It is harmony what you seek; then, we had better start training for it. It will not dawn on you automatically. It is a hard learning process.

It is noticeable that once one gets into a negative cycle when one cannot reconcile his demands; the feeling of frustration further builds in and spoils all forms of communication.

This negative feeling is reinforcing.

For your own sake and for those around you, it is best you break this cycle and come out a winner. The figure given below depicts the entire issue of the conflict cycle.

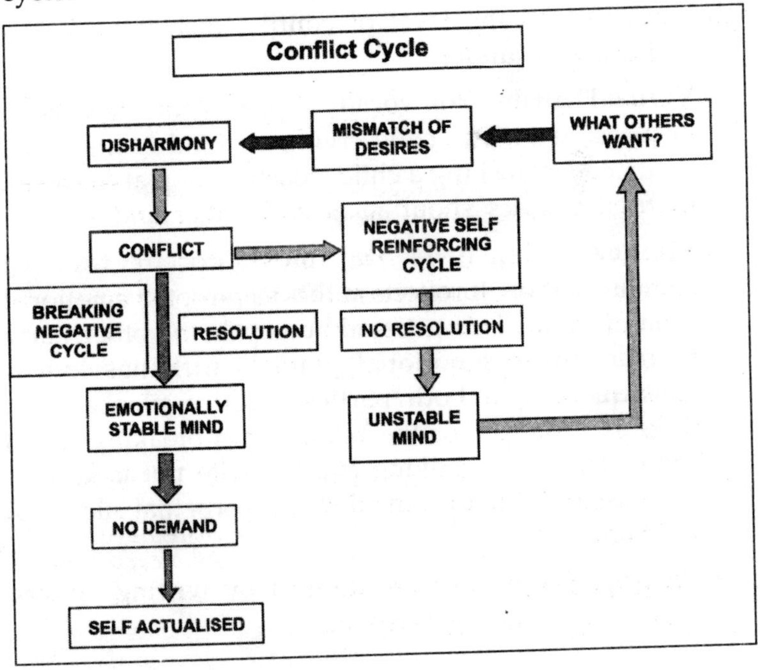

Though the conflicts based on communication deficiency are vast in scope, let me start with a simple moot point, of what do we understand of the word conflict in first place.

CONFLICT

Conflict can be termed as, the divergence in opinions, shared views and matters, which effects the smooth functioning between the individuals, people, sections of the society and nations. They are also the, situations of discord and disharmony, discontent and disillusionment. Over here, one can coin so many near meaning definitions, but the above underlying principles remain same – disharmony and discord.

Expressing Conflict

The expression of conflict also has various forms. It quickly jumps from the emotional mental state to show physical one, as the level of conflict increases. A few examples are as under:-

- **Verbal Diatribe.** You vocally express your displeasure or pleasure such as child crying for food or attention, mother admonishing a child, coach yelling at his team, married couples shouting at each other and so on.
- **Silence.** Silence is the most potent tool of communication. It reflects at the deep-rooted emotional state of mind. This generally compels the other party to react in an emotional plane, which has longer consequences. If both parties practice silence, then there is a danger of the relationship breaking down completely e.g. a sulking child, a wife not talking to her husband due to some discord, perpetual silence of the boss,
- **Writing.** People express discord by writing, letters, messaging, sending cards etc.

- **Body Language.** Then there is the body language to express discord. The combination of posture, limb, and gesture and eye communication also express conflicts in varied ways, for example a defeated team, a dejected child walking, a community dance of happiness and joy, tribal war/hunting dance reflective of seriousness; near-total detachment, sad eyes, aggressiveness; it can be both mental or physical: ultimate outcome is violence. The ultimate of violence is war.

The question originates why there is a war between two nations. I will explain it as simply as possible: there is an issue; to resolve the issue they hold a dialogue; the dialogue fails; both the contending parties harden their stances; egos inflate and to satisfy their egos interlocutors plunge the respective countries into war.

Who lost?

Soldiers and the society.

Who won?

Neither of the warring countries.

What was lost?

A mutual agreement through dialogue.

How will it ultimately be resolved?

Resolution will emerge through direct dialogue or through a mediating party.

What is interesting to note is that war was the outcome of the dialogue failure. Now we believe that the resolution to war will emerge from dialogue. Now I would request you to please shut your eyes and think for a few seconds, where in all things between you and others have gone wrong. Inescapable answer is that poor dialogue; pathetic national communication was responsible for the war.

CONFLICTS

Conflicts are of many types. I can broadly categorize them as under.

Personal Conflicts: A personal conflict is always due to one's own behavioural traits and own psychological profiling. Personal conflict can be with self, your ego, your desires, your wants, your other needs.

Organizational Conflicts: Here in two separate entities of business, tend to have a conflict. An organization per se is inanimate led by men and women who run it. Those people, these few individuals, in echelons of power, whose views and desires conflict with others set of people, who run another organisation. The same can happen on larger plane between nations. Individual also can here have similar problem with the organization, wherein his views are not heard.

Societal Conflicts: A societal conflict happens when an individual fails to establish a rapport between himself and the people around him. The causes are acquired knowledge base, learning, biases, prejudices, own views and apprehensions.

In the above types of conflicts, it is pertinent to focus on:

Who is fighting?

Is it the individual as an individual or as a part of a group?

Why is he fighting?

Is it the threat to his individual/group ideas and/or his communication dialogue passes the comprehension of others?

How will it be resolved?

The resolution will happen by itself or through communication dialogue; or else try finding another way.

Conflict Dialogue and its Components

Dialogue is an expression of intent, between two parties.

Its components include writings, memos, talk, body language and expressions. It would entail the idea; the message as postulated by you is understood and executed by both in mutual agreement and in the atmosphere of willing participation. In addition, when it does not happen, it becomes the cause of conflict. It should be pertinent to note that a meaningful dialogue helps achieve as follows:-

- Re-establish communication.
- Re-start the communication.
- Explore own ideas through communication.
- Perceive and understand others' view points.
- Check out own stand in relation to others.
- Table our thoughts.

The chart below explains the mechanics of resolution of any conflict. We always have varied options, but which option always has the better chance of a resolution are what you, as a rational man has to choose.

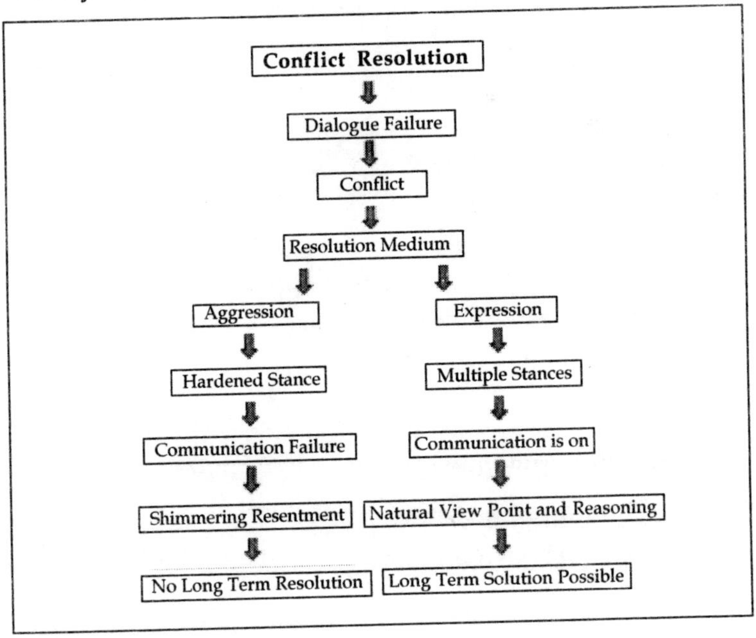

It is pertinent to remember that conflict is a very natural phenomenon. It has been existing since ages and will continue to do so for more ages. It will happen between individuals, organizations, communities, races, sets and nations. My only submission is that one should be open about it and work towards resolving it always.

Internal Exploration

- Check through the power of self-realization about your conflicts in your own life.
- Check with yourself with whom are you in conflict in life. Are they personal, organizational or societal?
- Check with yourself why you are in conflict.
- Check with yourself, why others are not in conflict with the same situation or person. What is their secret of no conflict?

Chapter - 5

Communication Cuts

"Conservatism stands on man's confessed limitations; reform on his indisputable infinitude; conservatism on circumstance; liberalism on power; one goes to make an adroit member of the social frame; the other to postpone all things to the man himself; conservatism is debonair and social; reform is individual and imperious."

—Ralph Waldo Emerson.

Effective communication is the ability to pass information from one person to another and ensuring that people have full idea of the contents the way they were originally packaged.

The communication is complete when it does not generate any back-queries and the intended work or action is complete to the full satisfaction of the sender. However, a feedback is necessary to see its implementation. The feedback is always obtainable from the sender. However, when did they understand your message in entirety? The anger with other, the very need to explain again means that there were communication losses in the process of transmission and reception. These losses or cuts make communication that more important a subject to study to that why they happen.

Effective communication is not as simple as explained above. Let us understand the queries set below:

- Why do your parents get angry?
- Why does your boss lose his cool?

- Why do not your friends see your logic?
- Some movies are enjoyable for others while you dislike those.
- Why do two brothers fight like wild dogs or sisters like wild cats?
- Why is the granny annoyed with her cutie pie?
- Why mothers-in-law are so fearsome?
- Some families live together happily.
- Why certain people sacrifice their lives for others?
- Why do few people stick together?
- Why do some nations fight as a bloc and others alone?
- Two business competitors are at loggerheads while the other two competitors help and complement each other.
- In a family of several siblings, two of the siblings have a deeper emotional bonding.

COMMUNICATION HARMONY

I had earlier spoken about communication harmony. Harmony is the natural state of things.

Studies on the subject have proved that genes produce frequencies and those frequencies, which match each other produce harmony. Any agitated matter, anywhere in the world, will come to natural state of harmony with its environment. Whether they destroy each other, live in each other's gravitational pull, or fuse together, they will find harmony of existence. Harmony of all external forces is the law and preordained order of existence to survive. Were there no harmony in environment, catastrophic order would have been ever prevalent.

In such a situation, *(a)* Could the life form grow without having a harmonious environment, having right quantity of minerals, water, light and heat? *(b)* Could the earth exist in the solar system without being in harmony of sun and other planets including our own moon? *(c)* Could the humanity flourish and grow without being in harmony with each other?*(d)* Humans have tried innumerable times to fight each other out of existence but it is the harmony of human nature, which prevails over insanity? *(e)* Could knowledge spread due to disharmony of thought? *(f)* Would you acknowledge Mozart, Zubin Mehta or *ragas* of lore as great had there been no musical harmony? *(g)* Would you have witnessed any heart breaking dance performance if the steps were not in harmony with music? *(h)* Will your child excel in exams if he is not in harmony with his knowledge? *(i)* If your marital relationship is good, it is due to harmony in relationship with your spouse; *(j)* Great teachers and orators always connect with their audience; *(k)* Great seers and sages are in communication harmony with their inner self and the feelings of the masses; *(l)* and you cannot communicate effectively without establishing a rapport with your audience.

The above questionnaire brings one issue to fore that communication harmony is essential to live happily. As mentioned hereinbefore, rapport between the speaker and the listener is paramount for communication harmony. Any misconception, misunderstanding, deviation or anger is a sign that communication did snap at some point of time.

We are facing communication cuts every day, knowingly and unknowingly. It thus becomes important that we know about them.

Let us refresh our memory with what are communication barriers.

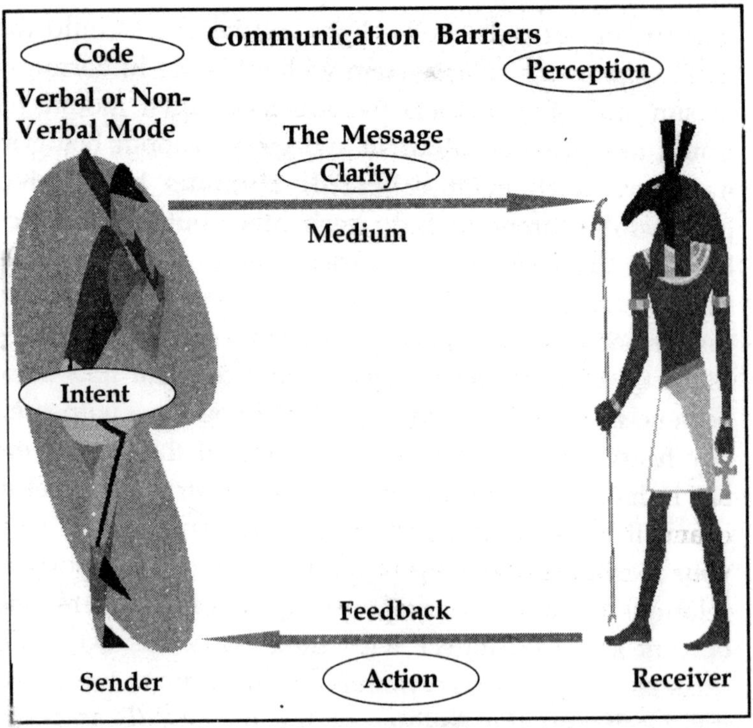

The instant diagram explains that communication cuts can occur at any of the five stages as follows:-

- **Intent:** What was the original intention of the message itself as sent by the sender? Was it pure in intent or had any hidden messages or other meaning, double meaning and interpretations. Example the word mate: it means a friend, low-grade worker and sexual intercourse.
- **Code:** What code you used in sending the message. Was it one, multiple or in part combination of two. When you speak and wink, it will convey a different message than when you only speak. Code is applicable to the receiver also when he becomes the sender of the action.
- **Clarity:** It means the number of physical media used, decision points, length of the message, physical snaps etc.

- **Perception:** It means the psychosomatic reception and assimilation of the message.
- **Action:** Is the resultant action as executed by the receiver, which has your expectancy attached to the value of the message sent earlier? The action differs due to host of psychological and physical reasons.

It only takes a few aspects to distort the communication message. The reasons can be million, but one reason is more than adequate to distort the message to an extent, that it becomes an afterthought issue of a debate, which could have averted or courted a disaster. Hence, it is important to identify the issues that can distort any communication message so that we are aware that such issues do exist. The figure, given below, points to various factors, which distort a pure communication message.

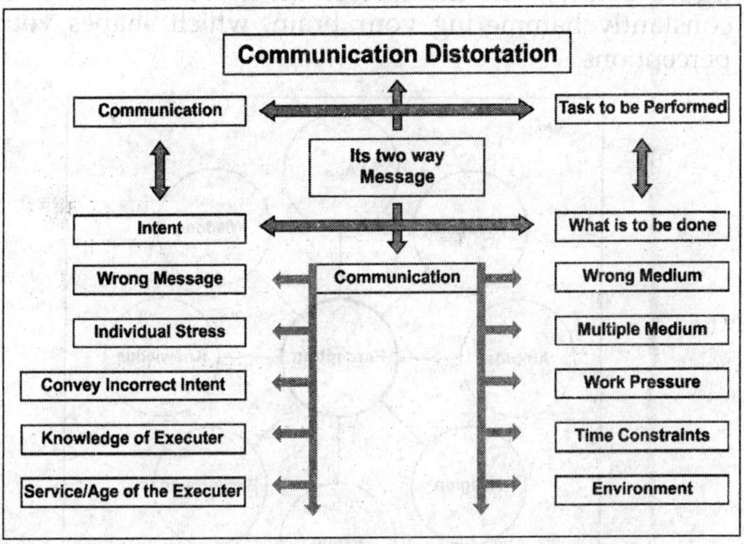

Having analyzed where in the entire process the communication loss, cut or barrier can take place, let us proceed to understand the reasons of these in more detail.

PERCEPTUAL CUTS

"To effectively communicate, we must realize that we are all different in the way we perceive the world and use this understanding as a guide to our communication with others."

—***Anthony Robbins***

We hear what we perceive.

We perceive what we want to hear or believe in.

Perception shapes immensely the way we communicate. It also shapes our intent and subsequent actions. It is the key ingredient of what you as an individual expect from the other party and see or judge he or she will complete your stated actions.

As discussed earlier, the perception is a combined function of several issues such as, age, wisdom, acquired knowledge, culture, family background, peer group, religion, attitude, imagination, thoughts at that moment and how well you radiate or imbibe communication (see figure below). All the factors as stated are inbound, constantly hammering your brain, which shapes your perceptions.

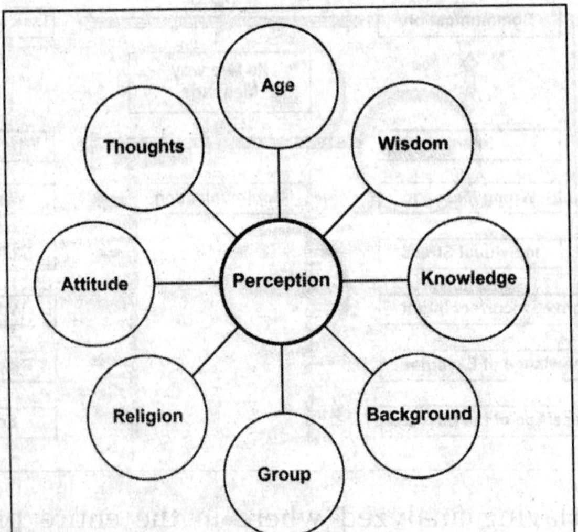

Let me explain this issue with the help of two examples.

First Example. I was posted in Arunachal Pradesh, bang at Bum La (it is a Pass on Himalayan Crestline) on Indo-Chinese border. This was a place the Indian troops had fought a very heroic but a loosing battle in 1962. We had reoccupied the territory and the area still remained disputed. I was there on the occasion of opening the first border meeting hut, for which the Chinese had agreed. The orders had been passed down to make a border hut, within a week, on the perceived border. Let me give you the various perceptions of the parties involved.

- ***The Lieutenant manning his platoon above the Pass***. The Indian Army could not house him in a comfortable bunker and here they were making a fabulous insulated five star barrack for fun and frolic of a quarterly border meeting that too with the enemy.
- ***The Commanding Officer of the Unit***. Thank God, that he would not have to move his resources, in men and material, every quarter to make a tented camp.
- ***The Commanding Officer of the Neighbouring Unit***. Thank God, the entire muck was not his baby to execute. (I was this guy).
- ***The Chinese***. Hey guys, we wanted a small hut and not a five star hotel.
- ***The General Officer Commanding***. It will show the enemy how fast we can mobilise our resources; hence, in war, we will only do it better. The days of unprepared Indian Army of 1962 were over.
- ***The Commander of the Army***. Of the entire disputed border delineation line, the Chinese had agreed to this place, thus this stretch was now officially recognised, thus not under any dispute.

Communication message was one; make the hut and action was to make the hut but the perceptions were many to why it was being made. *Despite different perceptions, the communication demand was met.*

My **Second Example** is a bit bizarre. In military teachings about communication gaps, there is a classical reference to **My Lai massacre**, which was perpetuated by a United States Charlie Company of 1st Battalion in Vietnam. I will just give you the gist of it.

- The message was to neutralise the Viet Minh fighters in village of Son My which had sub clusters of My Lai. The operation was planned from the intelligence as gained by **division intelligence** staff and Major General Sammuel W Koster, General Officer Commanding of 23 Infantry Division, made a plan *to neutralise the Viet Minh presence,* which had cost casualties to American troops. The message was clear in writing in evening. It went from, division to **brigade** where Colonel Dran K Henderson, Commander of 11 Infantry Brigade, planned the operation with orders *'to go in aggressively and wipe the Viet Minh there for good'*. At the **battalion headquarters of 1st Battalion of 20 Infantry Regiment**, Lieutenant Colonel F A Kanker, ordered *'to burn the houses, kill the livestock and close wells'*. At the **Charlie Company** briefing, Captain Ernest Medina, concluded in his orders that *'As all villagers go to the local market by mid morning, all left in the village will be Viet Minh or their sympathisers, they needed to kill all guerrillas, suspects including women, children and animals'*. The platoon commander of **number one platoon**, Second Lieutenant William Calley, on landing from helicopters near the target, next day by mid morning, without any opposition, *opened fire and swept through the village in a extended firing line, killing estimated 504 civilians.* **A classic case of disaster in communicating right intent and perception which got distorted it at every stage.**

How did the communication change into miscommunication?

- The last two channels were by air. Medium of message was changed. Distortion took place in the contents of the actual message, (intent and perception) at each channel/level of command.
- Situation was tense at the front with the platoon engaged constantly in battle for the last two months and the battalion had lost 28 men in operations. They were looking for revenge and a perfect operation came their way to vent their frustrations. Time given for analysing the situation was very less.
- The platoon leader who was stressed (actually a college dropout), thought he heard, kill and destroy all in My Lai. He opened fire without any provocation assuming all are guerrillas and set afire the entire village. From a simple message, to neutralise Viet Minh guerrillas in a village, the communication became, kill and destroy everyone in the village. Thus was born the famous My Lai cocktail.

Lessons drawn from above two examples.

If the correct perception of the communication can be told, the action becomes that much easier to accept and execute. In the first case perception was not passed down and people actually were in state of communication disharmony with the communications perception and intent in first place. However, as the task was simple, it was executed without any major ruffles.

The second case tells how perception is intensified and distorted by misreading intent. Intent was always clear, to be aggressive, so down the chain of accountability all maintained a very high aggressive intent. Fearing that their intent was not as aggressive as their General, all in the chain of accountability kept on increasing the amount of aggression until the original communication's intent was totally lost. Thus, interpreting intent wrongly will make you do a wrong action, which was not the part of the original communication intent.

For a good fruitful communication, thus it becomes paramount that the perception has to be in line with the intent of the original message. Any mismatch will not result in a complete communication.

Mind is the most glorious equipment in the human body. The body may require physical rest but mind in any physical state is always working, thinking, analysing, making choices, dreaming and experiencing.

The state of your mind dictates what you want to perceive; training of your mind dictates what you want to perceive; the radiation and absorption ability of your mind dictates what you want to perceive; overcoming the natural antithesis to labour of the mind dictates what you want to perceive; your life experiences in knowledge gathering also dictate what you want to perceive; the environmental situation around you will dictate how your mind will perceive; the education you receive dictates how you will perceive situations.

Perception though is mind related is also affected by the communication message itself through the clarity of the message delivered; the time needed to analyse the message; the speed at which the message is delivered; the relevance of the message; the danger or the threat it poses.

Other Factors

Other environmental factors like, society, the group itself and their thoughts and beliefs on that particular subject.

The organizational culture: The way a Special Forces unit reacts to a situation given a message and the way another, say border guards unit reacts, differs in entirety.

Number of channels employed for the message to reach the destination. By channels, I mean, written, radio, telephone, personal verbal, etc by which the original message travels to the intended audience.

Number of decision points through which the message passes. We all have done this famous pass the verbal message exercise through the class. More the decision points, more the distortion.

Communications in military context will also cover risks involved (losing life or limb); importance of the objective/task; your ability to make difference to the operations; your confidence in self and your team abilities; how well you read your commander's intent or he influences the situation. If you get the perception of original message wrong, your subsequent communication action will be very wrong.

"I said at the interview I was honest and hardworking - I never said I was competent."

BIASES/PREJUDICES

Bias is a particular tendency or inclination one, which prevents unprejudiced consideration of a question. There are several definitions of prejudice but the most apt is unreasonable feelings, opinions or attitudes, especially of hostile nature directed against a racial, religious or national interest.

Prejudice is the first stepping stone for forming permanent bias. Therefore, they complement each other, close fitted, in a perfect circular reinforcing loop. They generate your belief and lastly how you think. How you think shapes your actions. The intimate thoughts shape your core beliefs and the core beliefs, are the thoughts, which apply pressure on your mind to act in a particular way. Let me give you a very simple example. Your core beliefs tell you that eating raw meat or insects is not a done thing for a civilized individual. Then when they present you with a food tray as such for your meal, your action will be to push the plate away, for it is repulsive to your core beliefs. The illustration below sums up the entire process.

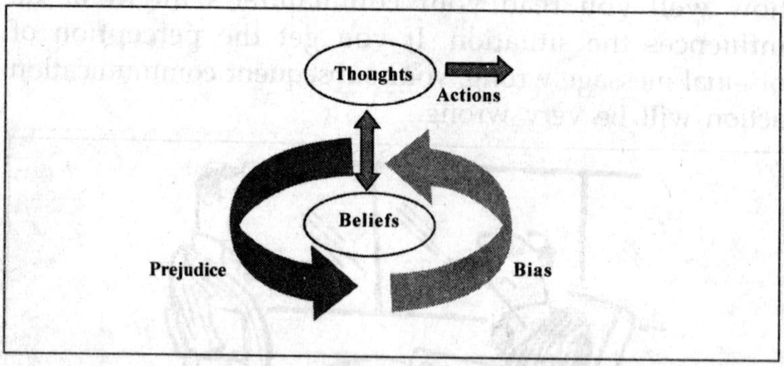

In very simple language, it means what you think about other things or how you relate your thoughts with things, which are ever prevalent in your environment and with those, you generally have active association. The association may be at personal level, societal level, work place, study place or at any other place. It is again your perception of things reinforced by your knowledge base, personal experiences, peer pressure learning; societal attitude, your personal attitude, colour of the skin; continental habitat, wearing habits, eating habits; financial status, your work, competitors in work and life; your likes and dislikes.

Let me give you some actual examples:

- Asians as successful managers was an unacceptable thought to European or Americans until Japan with its international conglomerates of Toyota, Mitsubishi changed that perception.

- Asians could never beat European troops in war, until a rag-tag army of Vietnamese troops drove the French out of Vietnam after giving a humiliating defeat to French troops in battle of Dien Bein Phu in 1954.
- Blacks could never equal whites in intellect until they proved it otherwise and latest Obama mania again proved it wrong.
- Women could not take effective roles in combat until Israel used them effectively in war.
- Sun will never set on British Empire and now that it has set, the empire is striking back economically.
- All terrorists in the world are Muslims, forgetting others who do it in the name of religion or political thought.
- Indians are stealing American jobs in Information Technology and America is losing, while the actual statistics show that it has given profitability to otherwise sinking American business, hence retaining the core American jobs.
- Muslims are not progressive, cannot be modern and do not take to education, while the most modern state established before Europe was born was Muslim Turkey.
- Why some do not eat halal meats, pork, beef, or frogs; in one part of the world these are delicacies while in other it is frowned upon. British called French, 'froggies', for they relished frogs.
- Rich rob the poor always, while maximum philanthropy in world comes from rich people.
- In the Indian context, Bengalis are very intelligent; Marwaris are money-minded; Punjabis are hard working; Keralites are keen workers.
- In Army's context, we base our views on certain observations or beliefs, which have no scientific basis

or historical data to prove that fact. As example, Gurkhas are great attackers/fighters (we know it is not entirely true) or Jats are great in defence (while they captured one of the most difficult targets in 1965 war) or martial races can only fight effectively (while bravery awards show it otherwise).

Such biases to any further effective communication, despite the best efforts of the sender. His message is not getting through despite his best efforts to radiate positively and constantly signalling that I am not what you think to be. In addition, the worst is that you do not want to think that he is what he is and he is what you think he is.

Bias thus becomes a good stopper of effective communication. Your earlier prejudice, reinforced in to your belief, will not let you hear the full communication. This bias block insulates your mind, like a negative aura around your brain, to receive any communication from an individual in its totality or face value, which is not in conformity of your beliefs.

Such issues, tempered by the brushes of prejudice/ bias, lead to great turmoil in organisations and in managing men effectively. It is responsible for distrust amongst a certain group of people, curtailing innovations, overlook in promotions, disparity in pay, creating an unhealthy working environment, encouraging sycophancy etc.

INTENTIONAL CUTS

In the previous chapters you had seen that how perception of an individual to an event and the given message enhances or curtails effective communication. Similarly, the basic intent of an individual receiving communication is the biggest obstacle in effecting communication. Therefore, you need to know what intent is: Is it the desire to do a task willingly? Alternatively, is it willing compliance to orders? On the other hand, is it state of your mind to do a task? Or, is it your physical and mental drive?

I think the right answer lies in combined sum of all the above observations.

We may describe intent as inner physical and mental drive of an individual to subordinate his beliefs or natural inertia to perform the tasks as dictated by a communication message. Alternatively, intent is the state of mind, your basic desire to do what you want to do. It may not have the willing component to execute task as per the communication message. Both these definitions of intent are right in their own context: one defines it being willing compliance while the another what you want to do. Whatever be the issue, it puts immense demand on us to understand its exact implications.

Given a communication input, if your intent is in negative to the given message, despite any subsequent supporting or threatening communication, the receiver will not complete the given task because you never intended to do the work in first place. You will make motions of doing work, feign illness, not be in right place and never get the needed information. Your safety and comfort seeking genes will overcome your rational sanity. You will feel tired (without work input), nausea (without sickness) and dizziness (without mental strain) in just to do work.

In the army, we come across many a time that cumbersome tasks become easy and vice versa. We can attribute it to the consonance of intent or dissipation of intent of participants involved. For effective command in any organization, army in particular, for timely and correct execution of tasks there has to be consonance in the intention of senior commander, the executing officers and the soldiers accomplishing the task.

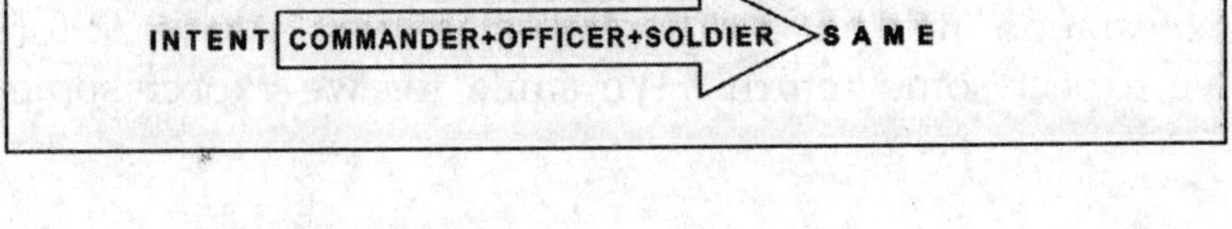

However, if we now analyse the previous My Lai massacre, we find that the above example holds good but the execution went woefully wrong. Aggression as an intent remained same along the continuum of intent line (see the illustration below). It is the case of Intent Multiplication, which distorted the contents of original intent. Therefore, retaining the original meaning of intent is very important in completing communication.

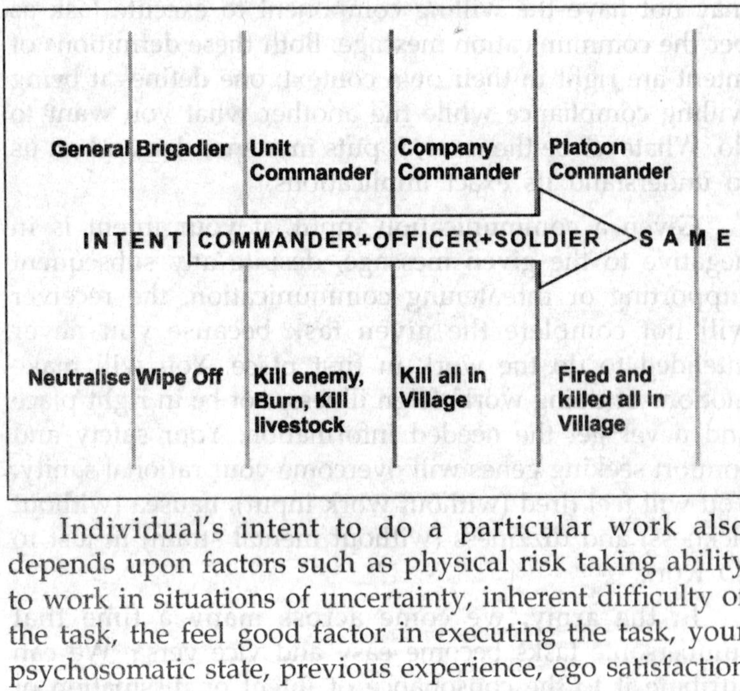

Individual's intent to do a particular work also depends upon factors such as physical risk taking ability to work in situations of uncertainty, inherent difficulty of the task, the feel good factor in executing the task, your psychosomatic state, previous experience, ego satisfaction mechanism.

EXPECTATIONS

We all live in our mundane lives with heaps of expectations. Expectation as defined in *Webster's Encyclopedic Dictionary* is the degree of probability of the occurrence of something. Expectation is nothing but an expectation. It is not a ridiculous statement. We work for we expect some returns. We smile for we expect some reward. We cry for we expect some attention. Expectations can be positive or negative in context. Positive expectations can be of love, sex, reward, praise, smile, monetary, knowledge enhancing or spiritual. Negative expectations are anger, fear, punishments, awards, or curtailment. We as parents have exercised both the positive and negative expectations and its accompanied emotions to control behaviour of our children. Some parents use positive expectations more and some negative. How your children communicate with you largely depends upon the mode you choose. Similarly, in all walks of life, where hierarchy is the order of things and societal laws are the order of life, your behaviour and communication get dictated by this sole aspect. People stay together or not stay together because of fulfillment of expectations or lack of it.

Let me explain.

- What does a wife expect from her husband: security, harmonious relationship, trust, love, support, her independence, importance paid to her thoughts and desires? Some will seek a bigger car, a bigger house, more fancy furniture or more jewellery. When there is a mismatch of expectations due to any cause, starts the first problem in communication harmony. If the communication disharmony is not nipped in the bud, the situation can deteriorate to divorce.
- Why do children leave their parents houses to stay separately in the same city, despite the comfort and love in their own home? There is mismatch of personal, peer group and society's expectations, of you as an individual, with your family unit. Where children reconcile their expectations they stay with their parents and where they cannot reconcile, they move out.
- In the corporate world why some companies willingly merge while, others do not. Some nations stick

together in war while others maintain distance even in peace. It is all about perceived expectations of each other and the benefits one will accrue.

I feel for a normal human being, looking forward to in life is having expectations from it. He does work day in and day out expecting some return. If there were no expectation of a monthly salary, would have he worked in any organisation? The answer is obvious "NO".

Thus, expectations become a driving force of your existence. Expectation is not only the physical aspect (pay etc) but mental in content also. If you are expecting to loose your life doing a simple task as dictated by a communication, most will not do it. Thus your psyche plays a crucial role in justifying your actions to your mind, that the communication is acceptable or not when weighed against the backdrop of expected payoffs. Despite dangers, thieves make it an art of stealing billions of dollars a year for the simple reason the expected payoffs are more than the physical dangers involved. Thus, if the communication conveys a demand, which is not in consonance with your expectations, it can lead to communication hiatus.

"Have you ever wondered why we call this the workplace, Harry?"

ASSURED ASSUMPTIONS

The human mind offers reasoning and logical choices. It generally makes a quick assessment of choices confronting him due to the communication demand. These choice assessments are a natural outcome of his previous knowledge, experienced similar situations, acquired knowledge and logical reasoning. I said so earlier that as a natural lethargy of the human to do mental or physical labour, it short circuits received demands to meet his own rationalized mental thoughts and actions.

We assume most of the time when we think and act on the following lines:

- I know better, for you do not trust the mental superiority of another human. It is a mental block, which manifests amongst a group or two set of individuals. Your ego does not allow you to accept the mental superiority of another individual.
- I am more experienced in that particular job. I know the entire process backwards. I know what to do.
- I am in a senior position due to hierarchical structure or age; therefore, I know what is good.
- I am of better social status due to the job, financial status or knowledge perception, or the institution you have acquired your knowledge. Classic example can be a financial corporate wizard; a Harvard graduate in ABN Amro, trying to listen to a man qualified in finances, may be from some college in Africa.
- Actual communication break due to physical distortion, unclear message and medium used where one has to fill in the gaps.

Let me again explain it with few examples.

- My Lai is my favourite case study. Why did Second Lieutenant William Calley assume that he was to kill everyone in the village regardless of age or gender, with, or without the lack of evidence of them being guerrillas – because he/she was an enemy? At each stage of policy formulation and planning, there was wrong perception, all the commanders in chain of accountability, filled gaps in information with reasonable assumption. The general thought the area to be full of guerrillas. He wanted to get rid of them. The brigade commander wanted the guerrillas wiped of his territory. The battalion commander's view was to kill a few suspects and torch the houses of their sympathizers. The company commander perceived all the villagers to be suspects and therefore expendable, including their homes.

- The army assumed that technology would prevail over the human adaptability and resourcefulness. Welcome to Vietnam where ill-equipped forces routed French, Americans and later Chinese.
- Indian political leaders took it for granted that no army can cross the Himalaya and attack India. China proved India wrong. It was something similar to what Hannibal did to Roman Empire by marching through Alps with his elephants.

When we assume, we always fill the gaps in information ourselves. We are afraid of cross-checking with others or the boss lest they think duffers of us. We want to look purposeful in front of others, especially junior who look up to us. We suddenly become very busy after receiving communication demand. You are in a tearing hurry to complete the job before they put more demands on our original demand. We think out a solution even before the process has started.

Thus, assuming is not as simple an exercise in filling the gaps in information by process of logical reasoning, elimination and selection of choices. It has the unpredictable human element attached to it and assumptions more often than not cause more breaks in effective communication that achieving tasks in the environment of uncertainty.

SELECTIVE LISTENING

Why do we always pick out our favourite music from cacophony of other noises?

Why can a mother hear her child's cry of distress from another room when several children are there?

Why do your children pick out the most embarrassing pieces of your communication, when you are whispering the same into the ears of your partners from a room across?

Blame it all on selective listening.

Selective listening is an art practised by all humans subconsciously to live in the noise harmony of your body and eliminate the noise pollution prevalent in the environment. This is when a person hears another but selects not to hear what they are saying of him.

Selective listening can take several forms and results in acting out in destructive ways. An example is to become passively aggressive by pretending to hear and agreeing to do what they said when actually your intent is not to act on the message, but make the other person think you will. Another form is to act on what you wanted to hear instead of what they said.

Researchers have found out that continued selective listening is the **precursor to destroy a relationship.**

Selective communication is most active when you are in a group or in a negative emotional state. One just refuses to listen what other is saying.

PERSONALITY BLOCKS

"Wise men talk because they have something to say; fools, because they have to say something."

—Plato

Any perceived behaviour that causes a mental, emotional, physical, or effect on another person is communication. Behaviour is an aspect closely connected to your personality. Your frame of mind gains mutual respect through giving or getting information, venting your emotions, reducing discomfort or gaining pleasure, maintaining mental stimulation.

Ensuring effective communication

- All involved in process of communication get their current needs met effectively and in totality well enough. You may give one candy to your five-year-old son, when he asked for it. However, his communication has not finished for he wants five candies and not one. You have not met his demands to his satisfaction.
- Between the parties concerned, it promotes self and mutual respect, trust, and shared satisfaction.

Anything, which hinders this, causes communication block. A few examples of communication block are as follows:

1. **Self Respect:** A communication implying that I do not respect you will never get through. The perceived voice and body dynamics usually decode such messages, unconsciously.
2. **Needs:** The communication fulfils a need. For example, I need to vent, and you need to persuade me to do something (take me from my perceived state of natural inaction to cause action). Every individual has some needs to fulfill. You may not be aware of your primary, secondary or surface needs. For example, "I want to talk to you" (surface need) may really mean, "I need to reassure myself you still care about me, because you've seemed distant lately."
3. **Mixed Signals:** Most of the messages and their words say one thing, and their face, body, and/or voice imply something else: e.g., "I'm angry!" said loudly with a smile and a coo will confuse a child whether he is being scolded for a perceived wrong action or being patted. The automatic responses to perceived double messages are confusion, and if habitual, increase the growing distrust of the speaker. The (unaware) speaker being controlled by two or more opposed sub-selves causes double messages. These are skills and true (vs. pseudo) from false self; generally, the sender is unaware that they are sending mixed messages.

Half the time we get on fine - the other half, he's here

4. **Distraction.** The other communication distracters are pain, thirst, sleepiness, headaches, worry, anxiety, or other strong emotions. Noise, flickering lights, motions, your thoughts, clutter of your work place, temperature also distract communication. Interruption too is a communication distracter. Interrupting your partner implies "I have a superior" message. Interruptions can imply self-importance and an inflated ego.

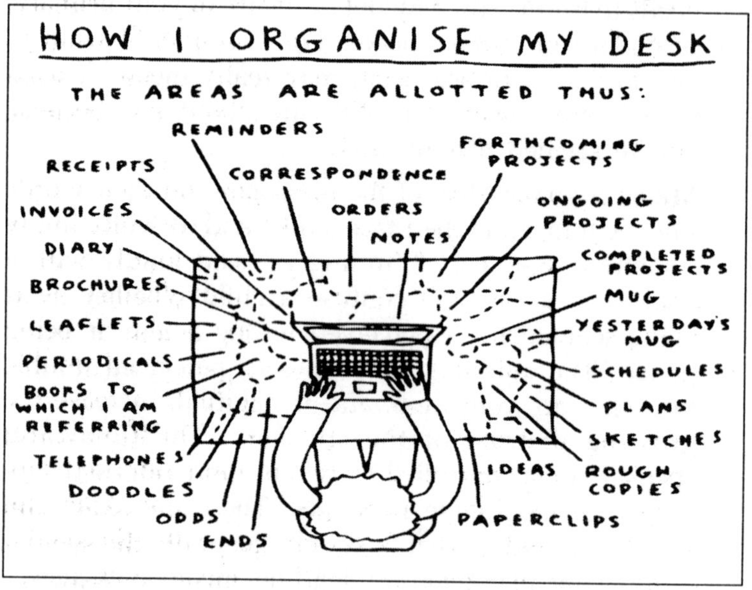

5. **Mind Reading:** This is an unconscious or an intentional way of discounting the other: "I know what you really feel or mean, no matter what you say (or don't say)." This often evokes defensiveness, resentment, counterattack, or withdrawal and denial. Blown up mind reading manifestation happens when the receiver starts talking before the speaker finishes because they "know what he (the speaker) is going to say."

6. **Current Emotional State:** The receiver may feel they should be interested, when they are really bored or distracted. Even when sent "skillfully," such denials

usually result in a sate of, "words may lie, bodies and faces do not". If habitual, such denials and deceptions breed confusion, and erode trust in the speaker. Children are especially quick to sense these aberrations. The following compound this as stated under:

- The receiver may be doing something that makes the sender feel unsafe in honestly sharing their current feelings.
- The sender may be emotionally unaware of this, or denying it.
- These are often uneasy identifying expressing emotions like hurt, fear (anxiety), confusion, guilt, shame and sadness. If frequent and ignored, withholding emotions hinders effective problem solving and strangles intimacy.

7. **Focusing:** A special case is when someone imagines a future event so vividly that they react to their partner in the present as though the imagined event had already occurred ("I know you'll be late again!") This is a sure sign of false-self dominance. This results generally in unbalanced and shallow communication. At worst, the receiver may

- Feel used, ignored, and resentful.
- Feel encouraged to ignore you.

8. **Spontaneity Syndrome:** This occurs when one person requests or demands something from another that can only be given spontaneously like trust, love, interest, acceptance, appreciation, desire, and respect. If the second person tries to comply, the first person may then say - "You're just doing that because I asked you to, not because you really mean it." Ah, it is a classic catch 22 situation. Do, be damned and not do then again be damned. A few apt examples are:

- "You never say 'I love you'".
- "I demand that you respect my wishes!"
- "You need to respect the sacrifices I'm making for you".

- "I need you to (want to) initiate sex more often".
- "You need to slim down".
- "You have to study harder".
- "Nothing comes free in life".
- "You are useless."
- "You are a cheat."
- "You are shamming."

9. **Generalizing:** This can effectively curtail the process of understanding and problem solving. You are always insensitive and inconsiderate!" Hence, they will receive differently than "I'm mad and frustrated because you're 40 minutes late and I missed my ride!" Your utterances imply the receiver is inferior and invite her or him to feel and be defensive about many past events as well as the present one. Normal responses to this block are defending, explaining, shutting down or counterattacking. For example:-

- "You did that."
- "I did not do that."
- "I don't know."
- "I did that because I thought..."

10. **Preaching or Moralizing:** Every individual at some stage in life starts preaching. You want to share your wealth of experience, your better knowledge. The receiver in first case has never asked for it and it shows him in a poor light as an illiterate. "I'm just trying to help!" can erode relationships if the receiver just needs to vent (be respectfully heard and empathically accepted) against the need to be "fixed." Uninvited "helping" can indicate a false-self compulsion to and may imply: I know how to fix your problem and you don't." How common it is for over busy, unaware parents to "fix" their child's problem before ***listening*** carefully, and considering if the best long-range help would be to encourage the child to identify and fill their own needs. Choosing this option will build a child's competence and self-confidence over a period, even if it frustrates them now.

11. **Sarcasm:** Being sarcastic to the colleagues erodes the receiver's self-esteem and is at the odds for cooperative problem solving. "You are an idiot, stupid, lazy, work avoider, weird, hopeless, a jerk...etc. This verbal communication conveys massive scorn, disgust, indifference, or rejection. Sarcasm is one of the biggest contributors in blocking effective communication. Sarcasm does the following.

- It dehumanises the individual.
- It shakes confidence of others.
- It marks a man rightly or more often wrongly.
- It throws intent of other being useless.
- It tells that you are not intelligent.
- It breaks your self-belief.
- It creates bad working atmosphere.

No, No, No! FIRST THE ROMAINE, THEN CROUTONS

12. **Withdrawal:** Physical or emotional withdrawal is a very powerful communication, very much akin to power of silence. However, it may imply "You scare or overwhelm me": or "I don't care about you and your needs now," or "I'm superior". This way, the abandoned partner will probably feel hurt; if the withdrawer denies or does not talk about leaving.

13. **Threats:** Threats usually provoke hurt, resentment, defiance, and everyone feeling badly about them. They also spoil the interpersonal relations on the individual plane and vitiate office atmosphere. Person, who uses threat to get work done or sends messages of action, has low self-esteem of him and is highly egocentric.

14. **Habitual Habits:** Certain self-repeating habits block the effective communication emanating from the sender. They so irritate the receiver that he ceases to take cognizance of it. These could be:

- Avoiding eye contact. This encourages discounting by the receiver for he sees you untrustworthy.
- Constantly apologizing, cursing, or speaking hesitatingly.
- Talking non-stop – not allowing anyone else to take the floor. All must listen to no one and me for I am the best and the only authority on the subject. This aspect induces poor listening in receiver and leads to ineffective communication. This happens most at teacher-student level.

15. **Information Overload**: Some individuals want to be the node of information and need it to boost this ego desire. This block often happens when the ego of the speaker controls him; he does not trust others, over-centralizes his work and does not delegate work to others; needs to vent, lecture, or moralize; and considers others inferior or incompetent.

16. **Argumentative:** Research shows typical males and females differ, often sharply, over which priorities to focus on in an interpersonal situation. For example, average females focus on relationships, cooperation, social harmony, feelings, and understanding, while typical male brains instinctively focus on logic, information, "fixing" things, power, and winning. Most of these characteristics are biological with a social fillip. Ideally, males and females recognize, accept, and use these complementary differences together, rather than trying to convert each other.

ARGUMENT AND DISPLAY OF ANGER IS WORST TYPE OF COMMUNICATION

It would be difficult to summarize the supra in entirety. It would have stood out that communication or lack of it is the result of how a man develops into an individual for total interaction with the society. That interaction firms his beliefs and shapes his personality, which furthers the communication in its own peculiar way.

The communication message also originates many options of what is the right way to proceed, too many options and all the right and good ones are available. (Refer the figure below). It is the choices you make and sticking to them with conviction to complete the given communication messages demand.

You better choose your own path and do it fast,
Or thou in this demanding world will not last.

INTERNAL EXPLORATION

- Just close your eyes and think what type of personality you display. What are your specific personality traits? Were those an obstacle in your endeavours to communicate?
- What are your perceptions, biases, and prejudices about each individual in your office? Are your perceptions genuine or preconceived notions
- Have you always stated your intention clearly and precisely to those working under you? If not, why? Is it due to the lack of vision and thought clarity on your part?
- What are your expectations from your peers, juniors, bosses, organisation, your loved ones, your wife and children? Do your expectations synchronize with their value system? Do they need to change to your standards or you modify your expectations?
- Do you indulge in selective listening? Is it the lack of time or those others are not up to your knowledge base?

Chapter - 6

Communication Shine

"The single biggest problem in communication is the illusion that it has taken place."

—George Bernard Shaw

In a jewellery store when you are staring down at numerous diamonds, the one and the only one you want to present your wife, your eyes automatically lock the most lustrous one. Well the cost does make you choose the dullest one but then it is entirely a different matter. Here we are talking about communication. The ability to outshine and be noticed stands out. Well in the process of dealing with communication per se, to outshine to get noticed is one major part, the other one's being, ability to deliver, perceive, analyse, judge, rectify and harmonise. Let us see how we can maximize our communication output. According to the experts, one can communicate effectively when one understands the stages of interpersonal communication, which are explained below:

The Phatic Stage: This begins with the greetings and accompanying gestures such as eye contact, the smile, etc. In a formal encounter, there is more distance between the individuals, as compared to in the case of an informal encounter. This stage is the warming-up stage. There is no meaning and intention, but just the setting for the next level of the conversation. This sort of communication happens between people who you meet on not very regular basis and even if you do, there is some difference in status and position.

The Personal Stage: This is the second stage in which the individuals bring a more personal element into the conversation. During this stage, one generally brings down their social guard and begins to interact more openly. They are ready to let the others involve in the conversation more about themselves and the hesitation decreases. Interpersonal interactions generally move into a third stage. It is the type of communication found amongst old colleagues and old friends.

The Intimate Stage: This stage of communicating usually involves opening one's heart and sharing rather intimate details, which is not a part of professional conversations, e.g. communication between husband and wife or between lovers. Keeping in mind these stages, one becomes more aware of how their conversations should progress and where they need to conclude a conversation, or extend it for that matter.

The overlapping and mixture of these stages brings forth the various types of communications as experienced between human beings as explained in the figure alongside. The combination of different types of communications between two different parties will create their own unique type of communication. We can generally label them from the level of familiarity, personal understanding and intimacy. I am sure there are many other means of meaningful communication but that is not the aim of the book. We as professionals have to find our own test bed of the best form of communication, as illustrated in the diagram.

Stage of Interpersonal Communication

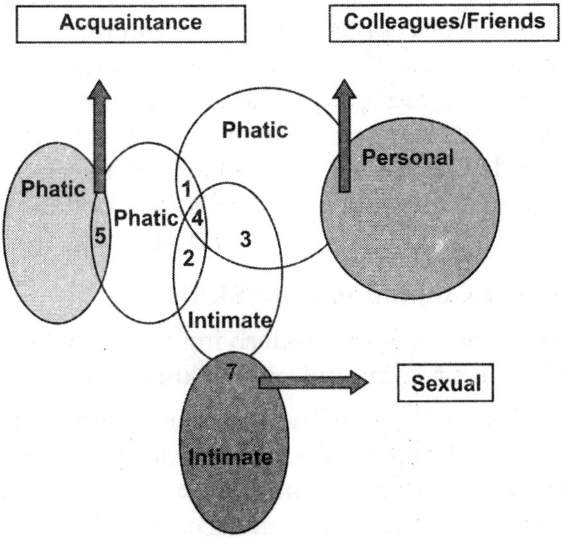

1. Business like communication professional and ethical
2. Platonic communication, strong likes.
3. Lovers communication, sexual oriented.
4. Best communication if sexual intimate overtone removed.
5. Acquaintance communication.
6. Mature colleagues communication.
7. Sexual communication.

COMMUNICATION ABILITY

The ability to communicate is the primary factor that distinguishes human beings from animals. The ability to communicate better gives an edge to the better interlocutor. This is also the key factor, which, differentiates between a better speaker, more effective boss, better parent etc. Thus, it is essential that one should be an articulate communicator because it makes all the difference between personal and professional life.

In order to develop these precise communication skills, one need to acknowledge the fact that we need to improve our communication drawbacks from time to time. We need to take stock of the way we interact with the environment and the direction in which their work and personal relations are going. The only constant in life is change, and the more one accepts one's strengths and works towards dealing with their shortcomings, especially in the area of communication skills, the better will be their interactions and a better social standing.

Importance of Communication Skills

The quote below is the underlying factor that explains the importance of communication skills.

"Identification is one of the key ingredients of effective communication. In fact, unless your listeners can identify with what you are saying and with the way you are saying it they, are not likely to receive and understand your message."

In fact, there are other such quotes, which explain the importance of effective communication skills: "Good communication is as stimulating as black coffee, and just as hard to sleep after."

Have you felt or left behind stimulating experience on more power of communication any time?

- Were you ever moved by a communication?
- Did a communication ever shake your core beliefs?

We will read another quote below:

"The newest computer can merely compound, at better speed, the oldest problem in the relations between human beings and in the end the communicator will be confronted with the same old problem, "of what to say and how to say it."

The major misunderstanding of our times is the assumption that insight will work with people who are unmotivated to change. Communication does not depend on syntax, or eloquence, or rhetoric, or articulation only; but largely on the emotional context wherein one hears the message. People can only hear you when they are moving toward you. It is for you to connect with them. Even the choicest words lose their power when overused. Attitudes are the real figures of speech, for they define the moment, that precise are when you are waiting to listen. Remember to listen attentively when someone is speaking. The problem with communication is the illusion that it is complete. The right to hear does not automatically include the right to take it seriously. Argument is the worst sort of communication.

Having thrown so much of Jargon at you, now let's see why communication is so important. I can summate a few lines and I am sure your heart and mind would have many more answers:-

- It connects people.
- It makes you heard.
- It makes them heard.
- It kick starts work/action.
- It completes the desire.
- It teaches.
- It makes you acquire knowledge.
- It humanises you.
- It completes you as a human being.
- It makes you a member of a society.
- It makes you a beloved.
- It makes your presence felt.
- It helps to coordinate.
- It helps in effective team work and team building.
- It helps you to deliver/reach your targets and aims in life.

BE AWARE OF COMMUNICATION PROCESS

Sorry if I am sounding repetitive, but to need to work on your communication short-comings one always has to understand and go through the entire thread of communication process, right from its basic knowledge as a studied subject. This remains the central essence to understand communication. One should always be aware of the communication process. One should be aware of every aspect of the present communication:

- The purpose
- The objective
- The need/requirement
- The positive feedback (what you actually expect).

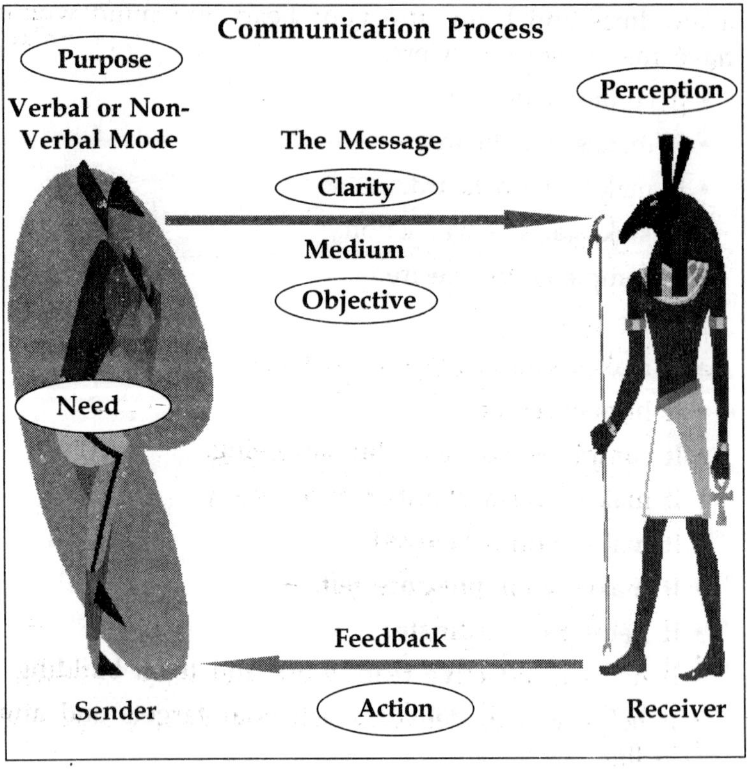

COMMUNICATION EFFECTIVENESS

"Effective communication is 20 percent what you know and 80 percent how you feel about what you know."

—Jim Rohn

Effectiveness of any programme and even any aspect of communication stems out from the positive feedback. However, to make your communication effective you need to generate a positive feedback. It is confusing even as it sounds simple. It is confusing if you are only bothered about the positive feedback. That anxiety can kill communication. It is simple if one concentrates on the content and method of delivery to make it comprehensible and interesting. With such a frame of mind, the feedback invariably will be positive, thus making your whole communication process effective.

The way one communicates does not only have an impact on their own profession and personal relations, but also an effect on others. Those who do not have appropriate communication skills are usually ignored or simply kept at bay whereas those with good communication skills are looked upon and well respected. After all a good listener and a good orator are popular in their groups, professional and personal.

We have seen it numerous times in our service days, that the presentations, briefings are given by "those" who have better oration skills. I have often heard the quip, **"This is all the manner of speaking English".** Well that is not true and a looser always will have something to say on it repeatedly, than to repeatedly trying to work on his precise shortcoming for his own betterment.

Teaching communication skills can be a rather daunting task, considering that almost every individual feels that they are very good communicators. In fact, most trainers prefer to be regarded as facilitators, who are able to bring to light the nuances that occur while communication ineffectively, rather than pointing a direct finger and saying, "You all cannot communicate well". Moreover, when this occurs the participants are ready to delve deeper within, bring out the negative aspects of their communications, and replace it with the positive corrective measures. Based on the communication skills training programmes conducted by known experts in the field, here are some tips to good communication skills as follows :

- **Maintain Eye Contact with the Audience:** This is vital, as it keeps all those present involved in the conversation. It keeps them interested and on the alert, during the course of the conversation.
- **Body Awareness:** For instance, if there is anxiety rising during the course of a conversation then one feels thirsty and there maybe a slight body tremor. At that point, one needs to pause and let someone else speaks. A few deep breaths and some water works as the magic potion at such a juncture.
- **The Message:** Are you sending the right message? Ask that yourself repeatedly. Is that what someone actually wants to hear?. Most of the times we are caught just sending a wrong communication message.

Most of the time I am wondering that **am I sending the right message**? Is that what someone actually wants to do? (Refer the figure below). Most of our times we are caught just sending a wrong communication message.

"What is it, boy? Want to go outside?"

VOICE CULTURE

"Take advantage of every opportunity to practice your communication skills so that when important occasions arise, you will have the gift, the style, the sharpness, the clarity, and the emotions to affect other people."

In the case of verbal communication skills, voice plays an important role. After all, one maybe knowledgeable in their domain area, but conveying their knowledge may seem like a mammoth task. This is the reason why, as a part of communication skills training there is ample emphasis laid on voice culture. Ever wonder why we love harmonious melody and not harsh discordant mixture of sounds. Well it is as basic as good and bad which we learn to differentiate from a very young age. Some issues that improve your listenable melody are:

- One aspect of culturing the voice is understanding intonation. This is the rise and fall in pitch, which occurs as we speak. There are various patterns of intonation. For instance, there is singsong, monotone, jump up and step down, etc. When one intonates one puts music, melody and rhythm into the way, they speak.

- Intonation follows certain guidelines that help one decide which are important and key ideas on which one needs to rise and fall in pitch. When one follows these guidelines, one can clearly communicate to the listener the important ideas in the message.

The following are the various other factors that help one to modulate well, gain correct intonation, inflection, and syllable stress.

- Be enthusiastic.
- Avoid speaking in a monotone.
- Exaggerate voice inflection.
- Pause to create effect.
- Pace between fast and slow.
- Modulate between high and low pitch.
- Bring power with the play of volume – loud and soft.
- Enunciate the words with clarity.
- Do not be repetitive.
- Do not mumble, murmur or fumble.
- Match the tone with attitude.
- Ensure 'idea impact' with usage of right words.

Trust

Though what I am going to write now, has no overt physical connect with your communication skills, but on an emotional standpoint, is the most paramount aspect which nurtures the quality of communication.

I would like to ask you one thing, whether will you ever communicate with an individual or a boss who has broken your trust with same previous level of openness or forthrightness? If your trust was once broken, the communication connect can never be re-established.

One can see varied examples almost as under:

- The way students open up and interact with the teacher they trust.
- Its how your child hides issues if his trust has been broken by his parents.
- Its how you suspiciously view your boss or colleagues if they broke your trust.
- It is the rapt attention and interest to totally emote with a speaker whom you blindly trust. The same trust pulled millions towards Gandhi or Martin Luther King.

Internal Exploration

- What is your self-assessment as an effective communicator?
- Compare yourself on scale of ten with best three effective communicators in your organisation. See where you stand in respect of delivering lectures and speeches or communicating effectively with others.
- Have you the courage to ask someone of your shortcomings? If you are shy, then self assess your shortcomings.
- What is the importance you give to effective communication vis-a-vis knowledge, wisdom, intellect and teamwork?
- What is your most effective tool of communication i.e. what is your communication strength?
- Most importantly, are you shining?

Chapter - 7

Polishing Your Antenna

"Do not wait until everything is just right. It will never be perfect. There will always be challenges, obstacles and less than perfect conditions. So what. Get started with each step you take, you will grow stronger and stronger, more and more skilled, more and more self-confident and more and more successful"

–Mark Victor Hansen

I have discussed above that man is a communication antenna. We radiate and receive communication waves. In addition, by that logic alone, a human is like any antenna. Thus, to enhance our antenna's output, any high school physics student will tell you to keep the metal pure, increase the power source, keep it clean and polished and restructure its shape and design. When above facts are simple, so even simpler is the quest, that it is us, we ourselves who have to mould or change to better communication as follows:

ATTITUDE

"Success is not final, failure is not fatal: it is the courage to continue that counts"

–Winston Churchill

Before we embark on any other journey, to polish one's antenna or shine in total honesty, the desire or force within, which challenges you to change, comes from your attitude.

Now what is attitude?

Attitude in nutshell can be described as what do you feel about a thing, what do you think about a subject and the way you behave towards a given situation.

What you feel about a thing is your speech of your heart and emotions. It is how you will emote internally as a human. The pain, anger, grief, love, care etc all will fall into this category which will describe that you are part of attitude.

What you think about a subject and is the speech part of your learned brain acquired intellect. This is the rational part of your attitude. It tells you between right and wrong. It tells you what to do. It tells you to initiate or not initiate an action. It tells you to take or not take a decision.

The way you behave towards a given situation, is the speech of your body translated into action. It manifests in various forms as under:

- The way you lead your life.
- The way you work.
- The energy levels you display.
- The keen interest you take.
- You are lazy, chirpy, lethargic, energetic etc all is your body eminating your attitude.
- Some people run away from danger, some risk their lives to save others.
- Some give up in face of hardship while some carry on despite it.

All this is attitude

Attitude evolves over a period of time. It comes from the way: (a) you have seen your parents behave in person and with society (b) What you have imbibed from your family values (c) How your learning experience has been while interacting with the society (d) What are your personal expectations for self, others, job and life (e) What loss and gain analysis is acceptable to you as a person and lastly how adaptable you are in your beliefs.

Remember, you have this particular attitude (it could be good or bad, right or wrong) acquired by yourself. You acquire it as it became a subconscious extension of your repetitive habits. Habits are learnt over a period of time. So attitude action is a learnt trait. Hence, attitude thus can also be re-learnt, re-formed by training your mind and body.

Why do we train men for war? Why do we train officers? Why do we train commando's separately? Why certain colleges produce only elite? It is for the simple reason they re-train your personal self to form a new attitude which goes in consonance with the ethos of the organization, work culture, values and beliefs.

To polish your antenna: hence you have to change your existing attitude which has tarnished it in first place.

Do I need to say anything more?

MAKING A GREAT FIRST IMPRESSION

Earlier on, I have spoken about the importance of the first contact for the human embryo and of course later of the child within his mother's womb. Biology has proved how important that contact is for the subsequent development of the child and it shapes the way the child will interact with environment later for those first contacts are also the foundation stone of his character building. This is what exactly happens in your first contact with others on any plane, be professional, social or emotional.

It takes just a quick glance, may be three seconds, for someone to evaluate you when you meet for the first time. In this short time, the other person forms a general opinion about you. This is the first impression, which is irreversible and sets the tone for all the relationships to follow. Therefore, whether it is career or social life, first impression is very crucial. I offer you some useful tips to achieve as explained:-

- **Be on Time:** The person you are meeting for the first time is not interested in your "good excuse" for running late. Plan to arrive a few minutes early. Moreover, allow flexibility for possible delays in traffic or taking a wrong turn. Arriving early is better than arriving late, easily, and is the first step in creating a great first impression.
- **Be at Ease:** If you are feeling uncomfortable, this will make the other person ill at ease and that is a sure way to create the wrong impression. If you are calm and confident, the other person will feel comfortable in your company.

PRESENT YOURSELF APPROPRIATELY

Of course, the physical appearance matters. The person you are meeting for the first time does not know you and your appearance is usually the first clue he or she has to go on. However, it certainly does not mean you need to look like a model to create a strong and positive first impression. (Unless you are interviewing with your local model agency) The key to a good impression is to present you appropriately.

They say a picture is worth a thousand words, and so the "picture" you first present says much about you to the person you are meeting. Is your appearance saying the right things to help create the right first impression? You must practice the following:

- **Start with the way you dress:** What is the appropriate dress for the meeting or occasion? In a business setting, what is the appropriate business attire – suit, blazer, casual? In addition, ask yourself what the person you will be meeting is likely to wear. If your contact is in advertising or the music industry, a pinstripe business suit may not strike the right note! For business and social meetings, appropriate dress also varies between countries and cultures, so it is something that you should pay particular attention to when in an unfamiliar setting or country. Make sure you know the traditions and norms.

- **Personal Grooming:** Clean and tidy appearance is appropriate for most business and social occasions. In short, you should spruce yourself up according to the occasion. Appropriate dressing and grooming help make a good first impression and help you feel "the part", and so feel more calm and confident. Add all of this up and you are well on your way to creating a good first impression. Pay attention also to the following:
- **A Word about Individuality:** One can usually create a good impression without total conformity or losing your individuality. Yes, to make a good first impression you do need to "fit in" to some degree. However, when you express your individuality appropriately within that context, you are seldom a loser. In some organisation, you find a serious dolt and a gregarious person. Just be yourself.
- **A Winning Smile**: There is nothing like a smile to create a good first impression. A warm and confident smile will put both you and the other person at ease. So smiling is a winner when it comes to great first impression. However, do not go overboard with this—people who take this too far can seem insincere, or lightweights.

- **Be Open and Confident:** When it comes to making the first impression, body language and appearance speaks louder than words. Use your body language to project appropriate confidence and self-assurance. Stand tall, smile (of course), make eye contact, greet with a firm handshake. All of this will help you project confidence and encourage both you and the other person feel better at ease.
- **Small Talk goes a Long Way**: Conversation is a verbal give and take. It may help you prepare questions you want to ask the person you are meeting for the first time beforehand. Alternatively, take a few minutes to learn something about the person you are going to meet for the first time before you get together. For instance, does he play golf? Does she work with a local charitable foundation?
- **Be Positive:** Your attitude shows through in everything you do. Project a positive attitude, even in the face of criticism or in the case of nervousness. Strive to learn from your meeting and to contribute appropriately, maintaining an upbeat manner and a smile.
- **Be Courteous and Attentive:** It goes without saying that good manners and polite, attentive and courteous behaviour help make a good first impression. In fact, anything less can ruin the one chance you have at making that first impression. So be on your best behaviour. One modern manner worth mentioning is to switch off your cell phone. What first impression will you create if you are already speaking to someone other than the person you are meeting for the first time? Your new acquaintance deserves your full attention. Anything less and you will create a less than good first impression.

EMPATHIC LISTENING

"Our lack of compassion stems from our inability to see deeply into the nature of things."

—Lama Surya Dass

Have you ever identified with someone when you are listening to them? If you do, you understand them much faster and better. It entails the following:

- **It is Emotional Understanding.** Empathic listening is a structured listening and questioning technique, which helps you develop and enhance relationships through a stronger understanding of what is being conveyed both intellectually and emotionally. If emotions can be captured, communication reaches a new level.
- **Trust.** Honest and effective use of empathic listening helps you win the trust of team members, helping you address the root cause of problems rather than superficial but potentially damaging symptoms. Trust begets more trust.
- **Sympathy.** Sometimes, this ability to see beneath the surface of people's obvious behaviour can make the difference between seeming harsh and unsympathetic on one hand, and on the other being humane and well-respected. Sympathy slows your care and when someone is cared for the responds better.

JARGON BUSTING

"Words are, of course, the most powerful drug used by mankind".

—Rudyard Kipling

Jargon, according to COD, is words or expressions used by a particular profession or a group that are difficult for others to understand. A workplace is the preserve of jargon - not outside the workplace. It can provide useful shorthand to get across specific meaning quickly. However, the jargons can play havoc with effective communications. Let me expand this aspect as follows. How do we communicate without creating barriers?

Examples:

- "Look at these sales figures! – You know Tom, you cannot put lipstick on an ass. If we continue this mammoth strategic partnering paradigm, we might as well be milking a mouse with no teats. We have got to cut the innards of this supernova whale and return to our archetype of using customer-oriented discretionary values to make product reengineering decisions."
- "I do not know where family doctors acquired illegibly perplexing handwriting; nevertheless, they have extraordinary pharmaceutical intellectuality of counterbalancing the indecipherability of transcendentalist intercommunication's incomprehensibleness. What the world's greatest nincompoops seem to have got together to jack our sanity out of the drum".

If your head is spinning after reading that, you are not alone. The culprit is jargon. The use of specialised terms, idioms, expressions, acronyms and abbreviations those are understandable to only a select group of people. However, jargon becomes a problem when it stops people understanding your message. When you start using jargon (perhaps unintentionally) with audience not intended for, people will find it difficult to understand you. Even within the group the jargon is meant for, meanings evolve and newcomers misunderstand. Soon jargon can create barriers within groups too.

When Jargon creeps in?

Every profession, organization and specialised group has some peculiar vocabulary that can speed communication between group members. This is okay, if the meaning is very clear to everyone who needs to understand.

Sometimes people replace perfectly acceptable and understandable words with fancy, specialised jargon, seeking to impress their audience. These specialist words seem to hold some magical power that can make the speaker feel more intelligent or more knowledgeable. Unfortunately, the impression he or she gives may be a negative one, rather than the one intended.

Whatever the reason you use jargon, if it is out of place and the audience misunderstands, it can create a two-fold problem. Whilst you fail to convey information to them, you may convey a subtle, negative message that you have given little thought to your audience; and perhaps that you are insincere and not trustworthy.

Worse, you may never know that your audience has not understood—people often do not say anything if they mistrust you, or if they fear of looking unintelligent themselves.

What are the Jargon Traps?

Here are some common uses of jargon. Which ones do you use?

- **Communicating with others in your jargon:** You use jargon with the audience who cannot comprehend your words/phrases, what is the point in talking to them. You are wasting your breath and their time. Use jargon when it helps convey specialist information, and avoid it at other times. We do it all the time in army, within specialized groups etc. Let me quote an example: my wife hails from Lucknow and after marriage came to Punjab and inadvertently said after having one sumptuous meal, *"masti aa gayi"* (I am feeling inebriated/happy). Shock and silence followed her usage of the word *masti* because in Punjab *masti* means feeling sexually high.

- **Unthinking:** People often use jargon simply because they are not thinking and it becomes a bad habit. Jargon that is appropriate within your team or specialist group is often unintelligible to outsiders, such as your customers or members of your family.
- **Trying to Impress:** Jargon does not impress people. You are more likely to create the impression of "trying to impress" than "being impressive". Others may see it as insincere or irritating. One of my friends' daughters studying in a college in Delhi used a term, "jhant" to point out a useless person. Imagine her shock when she actually learnt the meaning is "pubic hair" of the word in Hindi.
- **Distracting from Facts:** Some people take recourse to jargon when they want to conceal the truth, lessen the magnitude of something, or make it sound more impressive. It is the best to avoid this practice because concealing the facts is difficult. Listeners can see through it.
- **Where to use jargon:** Use jargon with those who understand it, use it to any extent but not with those who cannot make head and tail of your utterances. Therefore, you have to decide where to and where not to use jargon.

Let's burst your Jargon

When it comes to communicating effectively, jargon often gets in the way. It creates barriers that stop people understanding you clearly and completely. To burst your Jagron, you must:

- Use simple, everyday language. Your communication will be more effective and more thoughtful towards your audience.

- It is always better to be clear than to be brief or 'clever'.
- Avoid the above stated obvious jargon traps.

COMMUNICATING IN A CRISIS

When a crisis or some other adverse situation occurs, the natural instinct is to close ranks, work furiously to contain the damage, and retrieve the situation to normal. We go into damage control mode to save our organization and ourselves. However, this approach can be wrong. We have all seen major companies terribly wounded when the press senses a "cover up." In addition, we have seen situations where gossip has spiralled out of control with damaging results. We have seen it in our service too so many times, when we make a hash of simple fact, for fear of openness.

When companies try to gag the official communication channels, communication does not stop. In fact, it can often increase and does increase exponentially by the hour, the period the communication is closed. The problem is that this communication can be full of rumour, innuendo, inconsistencies, half truths, and exaggerations. More than this, the employees and clients lose trust and confidence in the organization. On the contrary, when an organization is facing a crisis, the management should be open and honest; it should not hide any facts from its employees. During crisis period, observe the following religiously:

- Keep the media interaction short and simple.
- Do not sound and appear to be hysterical.
- Have one point interaction at fixed schedule. Only the nominated spokesperson should reply all the queries and not any available top boss or various bosses. Remember, more the number of people replying to the query more will be the confusion.

- Communication during crisis is a hallmark of a man. We have seen umpteen examples of men and juniors talking of a senior how he behaved under fire. The calmness, the conviction, the sound logic, the confidence with which he confronts situation when the bullets are flying and lives are at stake, makes such a man emulative.

ROLE PLAYING

Role-playing is a useful technique for thinking about difficult situations before they occur, so that you have good pre-prepared responses for the different eventualities that can arise. Role-playing helps to analyze problems from different perspectives, to spark brainstorming sessions, to experiment with different solutions to a problem, to develop teamwork, and help group problem solving. We in services do play a devils advocate to important briefings and presentations. This as reiterated above helps us achieve the following:

- Clarify our mind.
- To see through different situations.
- Keep us focused on job at hand.
- Plan contingencies better.
- Have adequate logical answers to any query.

Most importantly reshape our communication requirements in the light of new facts emerging out.

KEEP IT SIMPLE

I have studied thousands of battles and seen that only those battle of audacious attacks or stout defence were successful, which were dumb simple. In a complex world, simplicity is important. With so many things competing for people's attention, the more basic you can make something, the better. The more simple the message, the more impact it can have and the more likely it will be to attract someone's attention. **Details are never in short supply**. People typically look for details after something grabs their interest. But imagine if you started your message with most incomprehensible data and expected someone to smile at your acute knowledge. Let's take an example of Princeton University mathematics' professor trying to make grade fifth students interested in maths. Will he succeed by talking of algorithms? Or he would most probably succeed if he kept it simple. **Target the audience knowledge level and never display yours.** (Refer the figure on p.-150) To get them interested, though, you need to take a simple approach initially. Simplicity also helps in:

- Throwing out the correct intent of the communication. Everyone is clear from beginning of what precise is to be done.
- Least chances of misinterpretation. There is no fogging or clouding of the brain as message is clear.
- Being reacted to for action the fastest. The precise roles and tasks are known as the message is clearly understood.
- Keep people focused on their correct job and role, hence no wastage of effort by sheer duplication of tasks.
- Enable the audience to understand what you are saying.
- It enables most importantly the receiver send back the correct feedback. It enables correct and timely correction if need is so felt.

DELIVERING ARTICULATE PRESENTATIONS

Have you ever been to a really bad presentation or a lousy speech? It can be the most frustrating, boring and not a stimulating affair. If the information you are presenting is important enough for you to deliver orally, then it demands an appropriate amount of planning and preparation; therefore, the information you present is memorable and it is for the right reasons. Give a bad presentation and your listeners will remember you as lousy speaker. When someone presents and speaks well, it sends the message that the person is capable, confident, intelligent, and competent. These people claim your attention, which bodes well for your career. However, this does not come easy. You will have to do the following:

- Rehearse and rehearse until you become confident. Try speaking in front of a mock audience and before that in front of the mirror to check your expressions.
- Imbibe the voice culture and keep the facts simple.
- Have a confident and a positive attitude – remember no one knows the topic better than you do.
- Never read from a script, it shows how word–dependant you are on your script.

- Smile, interact, and be polite with your audience.
- The speaker should check and monitor his body manners. It looks so silly and ungainly, if the speaker keeps on twitching his nose, scratches his chin, or shakes his leg involuntarily.
- Lastly, it is very important that you keep the whole mumbo jumbo as simple and as compatible as the intellect of the audience.

ICE BREAKERS

Ice Breakers can be an effective way of starting a training session or team-building event or even a formal speech. It just simply helps people lower their millions of perceived barriers so they can start communication effectively. As interactive and often fun sessions run before the main proceedings, they help people get to know each other and buy into the purpose of the event. The secret of a successful icebreaking session is again to keep it simple. Design the session with specific objectives in mind and make sure the session is appropriate and comfortable for everyone involved. Consider using an ice breaker when

- participants come from different backgrounds.
- people need to bond quickly to work towards a common goal.
- your team is new.
- the topics you are discussing are new or unfamiliar to many a participant.
- as facilitator, you need to get to know participants and have them know you better.
- to lower the interpersonal barriers which people assume before the start of any event.

ACTIVE LISTENING

"Heaven is a place where the wicked cease from troubling you with talk of their personal affairs, and the good listen with attention while you expound your own."

—Ambrose Bierce

Listening is one of the most important skills you can have. How well you listen has a major impact on your job effectiveness, and on the quality of your relationships with others. We listen to obtain information, understand, enjoy, learn and most importantly to communicate.

Listening to Communicate

Given all listening we do, you would think we would be good at it. In fact, we are not. Depending on the quoted study, we remember a dismal 25 - 50 per cent of what we hear. That means that when you talk to your boss, colleagues, customers or spouse for 10 minutes, they only really hear 2½ to 5 minutes of the conversation.

Turn it around and it reveals that when you are receiving directions, you are hearing the whole message neither. You at best can hope that you have captured the important parts in your 25 - 50 per cent but it may not be so.

Therefore, it would be safe to assume that your antenna is not pure and not polished: for you are receiving less than radiated. If it happened to your mobile phone or any other scientific instrument, I am sure you would seek full replacement with full compensation.

Clearly, listening is a skill that we can all benefit from improving. By becoming a better listener, you will improve your productivity and ability to influence, convince, persuade and negotiate. What's more, you will avoid conflict and misunderstandings: all necessary for your professional and personal success.

The way to become a better listener is to practice "active listening". In order to do this you must pay attention to the other person. You cannot allow yourself to become distracted by what else may be going on around you, or by forming counter arguments that you will make when the other person stops speaking. Nor can you allow yourself to lose focus on what the other person is saying. All of these barriers contribute to a lack of listening and understanding.

Acknowledgement can be something as simple as a nod of the head or a simple "uh huh." You are not necessarily agreeing with the person, you are simply indicating that you are listening. Using body language and other signs to acknowledge you are listening also remind you to pay attention and not let your mind wander. You should also respond to the speaker in a way that will both encourage him or her to continue speaking, so that you can get the information if you need. While nodding and "uh huhing" says you are interested, an occasional question or comment to recap what has been said communicates that you understand the message as well.

BECOMING AN ACTIVE LISTENER

One can always learn to become an active listener by adopting five key elements of active listening. They all help you ensure that you hear the other person, and that the other person knows you are hearing what they are saying. Following can help you to listen actively:

1. **Pay Attention:** Give the speaker your undivided attention and acknowledge the message. Recognize that what is not said also speaks loudly.
    - Look at the speaker directly. Don't mentally prepare a rebuttal.
    - Avoid being distracted by environment.

- "Listen" to the speaker's body language. Refrain from side conversations.

2. **Show that you are Listening:** Use your own body language and gestures to convey your attention.
   - Nod occasionally.
   - Smile and use other facial expressions.
   - Your posture must be open and inviting.
   - Encourage the speaker to continue. Nothing stumps a talker or kills his desire to stop or impart his knowledge when he has faceless, expressionless and non-involved and non-appreciative listeners across. The game is played both ways by each other. You are attentive and show it, the teacher talks enthusiastically.
3. **Provide Feedback.** Our personal filters, assumptions, judgments, and beliefs can distort what we hear. As a listener, your role is to understand what is being said. This may require you to reflect what is being said and ask questions.
   - Reflect what has been said by paraphrasing. "What I'm hearing is..." and "Sounds like you are saying..." are great ways to reflect back.
   - Ask questions to clarify certain points. "What do you mean when you say..." "Is this what you mean?"
   - Summarise the speaker's comments periodically.
4. **Defer Judgment:** Interrupting is a waste of time. It frustrates the speaker and limits full understanding of the message.
   - Allow the speaker to finish.
   - Don't interrupt with counterarguments. Defer judgment and interrupting is a waste of time. It frustrates the speaker and limits full understanding of the message.

5. **Respond Appropriately:** Active listening is a model for respect and understanding. You are gaining information and perspective. You add nothing by attacking the speaker or otherwise putting him or her down.
   - Be candid, open, and honest in your response.
   - Assert your opinions respectfully.

     Treat the other person as he or she would want to be treated.

It is difficult to conclude the instant narration as the processes I have just narrated of honing ones communication skills, which are difficult to capture in few paragraphs, or touching on some few major aspects. I have just tried to refocus your thoughts to what can be done and what all can be achieved and what all one can do to change himself. In our life span, we have come across poorly dressed people, illiterate people, and people with no worldly knowledge but somehow they pack a verbal and a communicative punch that it keeps you glued to them like a bee to a flower. The power of communication lies within us and like the kingdom of God, which rests in our hearts and your soul, it is up to us how to take it out and shine in its goodness and glory.

Internal Exploration

- Is your antenna polished? If not what are the drawbacks, you have noticed.
- What are you going to do of the drawbacks you have noticed? To live with them as half the life has zoomed by is sure a lovely defeatist idea. It is never too late to learn and do something positive.
- How calm and agitated you get under stress situations? Do you require others help or are able to deal with it yourself?

- Are you a natural communicator or have you to rehearse it?
- Have you ever delivered an earth-shaking presentation, a speech or a talk, which got a standing ovation? If not, are you working for achieving one such?
- Do you blame your ineffective communication or your idiotic bosses for your lack of success in your life?
- Are you successful and happy when you refer yourself in comparison with your personal life and professional life?

Chapter - 8

Mind Games

"Whatever you hold in your mind will tend to occur in your life. If you continue to believe as you have always believed, you will continue to act as you have always acted. If you continue to act as you have always acted, you will continue to get what you have always gotten. If you want different results in your life or your work, all you have to do is change your mind."

The quest to control mind has been an old one. The science of Yoga has been one of the earliest directed to that purpose of controlling the mind through a perfect functioning of the body, which is in perfect harmony with nature. There is this ancient clamour to control mind but how can yoga or any other art control it when we do not know where in the body mind is. No scientific research has succeeded in pinpointing the seat of mind in the body. Mind is there but where in the body, nobody knows until this moment.

If you refer to the term mind games, it translates how one actually controls all his facets of mind and its resultant communicative actions to achieve his own stated goals. This concept formed the basis of earlier thoughts on spiritualism. To a modern scientist, he as always has broken it into more black and white and taken away the shades of spiritual cynicism. For them it is a 'passive aggressive behaviour' used specifically to demoralise or empower the thinking subject, often making the aggressor look superior.

How do you ever play mind games?

- You can play it if you have no mind of your own.
- You can play it if you do not know how mind works.
- You can play it if you do not know how to control the mind.

In this segment, which I feel is the superior culmination of the previous segment of 'Polishing Your Antenna', I will briefly discuss on the mysticism and the modernism, which can help you play mind games even better. Indian or eastern traditional thoughts referred to the culminating power of a mind as the foci of and free flow of energy from various parts of the body. The concept of Indian Body *Chakra,* or Chinese *Chi* or Japanese *Yen* all follow this principle in some applied form or another. On the other hand the modern philologist's propound it is a mixture of body, thoughts and interaction and influence of society as large. Let us dwell into the Indian system of total body self-control and harmonizing it with power of nature and thus subsequently the mind, which governs our actions. *Chakra* is a Sanskrit word that translates as "wheel" or "turning".

As a concept, it refers to wheel-like vortices, which, according to traditional Indian medicine, supposedly exist in the surface of the man. The *Chakras* are "force centers" or rings of energy permeating, from a point on the physical body, the layers of the subtle bodies in an ever-increasing fan-shaped formation. Rotating vortices of subtle matter, they are believably the focal points for the reception and transmission of energies. Supposedly, there are seven major *chakras* or energy centres or wheels of light located within the subtle body.

Diagrammatic representation of the seven *chakras* in a human body. Kangra School; late AD 18 c.

Paramhans Swami Maheshwarananda defines *chakra* as powerhouse in the way it generates and stores energy, with the energy from cosmos pulled in more strongly at these points. It runs along the spinal column in a curved path and cross one another several times. At the points of intersection, they form strong energy centres known as *chakras*. In the human body, there are three types of energy centres. The lower or animal *chakras* are located in the region between the toes and the pelvic region indicating our evolutionary origins in the animal kingdom. The human *chakras* lie along the spinal column. Finally, the higher or divine *Chakras* lie between the top of the spine and the crown of the head.

The seven primary *chakras* are:

Sahasrara is believably the *chakra* of pure consciousness. Its role is to communicate with the rest of the endocrine system and connect to the central nervous system via the hypothalamus. A lotus with one thousand petals symbolizes it. It is located at the crown of the head. The colour violet represents Sahasrara and it involves such issues as inner wisdom and the death of the body. Sahasrara's inner aspect deals with the release of *karma,* physical action with meditation, mental action and universal consciousness.

Ajna, also known as the third eye *chakra,* linked to the pineal gland, which may inform a model of its envisioning. The pineal gland is a light sensitive gland that produces the hormone melatonin, which regulates sleep and waking up. A lotus with two petals corresponding to the white colour, indigo or deep blue symbolizes Ajna. Mentally, Ajna deals with visual consciousness. Emotionally, Ajna copes with clarity on an intuitive level.

Vishudha relates to communication and growth through expression. This *chakra* is located near the thyroid in the throat. A lotus with sixteen petals symbolizes Vishudha. The colours light or pale blue or turquoise is characteristic colours of Vishudha. It governs self-expression and communication, as discussed above. Physically, Vishudha governs communication, emotionally it governs independence, mentally it governs fluent thought, and spiritually, it governs a sense of security.

Manipura controls the metabolic and digestive systems. This *chakra* supposedly corresponds to groups of cells in the pancreas, as well as the outer adrenal glands and the adrenal cortex. These play a valuable role in digestion, the conversion of food matter into energy for the body. A lotus with ten petals corresponding to yellow colour symbolizes Manipura. Physically, it governs digestion, mentally personal power, and emotionally expansiveness.

Anhata relates to the thymus, located in the chest it enhances the immune system. A lotus flower with twelve petals and related to colour pink symbolizes this *chakra*. This *chakra* involves complex emotions, compassion, tenderness, unconditional love, equilibrium, rejection and well-being. Physically, it governs circulation, emotionally unconditional love for the self and others, mentally passion, and spiritually devotion.

Swadhithana corresponds to the testes or the ovaries that produce the sex hormones associated with reproductive cycle. A lotus with six petals corresponds to the orange colour symbolizes this *chakra*. It deals with relationships, violence, addictions, basic emotional needs, and pleasure. Physically, Swadhithana governs reproduction, mentally creativity; emotionally it governs joy, and spiritually enthusiasm.

Muldhara is concerned with instinct, security and survival and to basic human potentiality. This *chakra* occupies the region between the genitals and the anus. There is a muscle located in this region that controls ejaculation in the sexual act of the human male. A lotus with four petals and red colour symbolizes Muldhara. It governs sexuality, lust and obsession. Physically, Muldhara governs sexuality, mental stability, emotionally sensuality, and spiritually it governs a sense of security.

Now how does the practice of these issues help you to perfect your communication?

A few advantages that I can think as a nonprofessional are:

- It increases your concentration.
- Your body will be healthy, fit and vibrant.
- You can direct your actions by controlling your thoughts to behave in a positive and a healthy way.
- You will exude radiant energy of goodness.
- You will be in tune with the environment and vice versa.

- There would be minimal effort required on your part and minimum friction within the environment.
- You will exude pure communication.
- It will rejuvenate your mind.
- It will rekindle your subconscious to do good always.

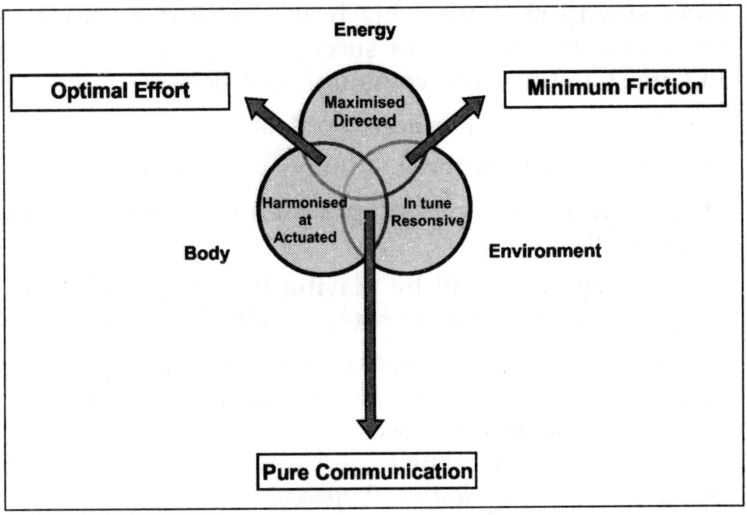

I am no self professed authority on the functionality of *chakras* but I am firm in belief that systems which were being evolved even thousands of years ago would give you benefits of a healthy body. What does an actualised and a body harmonised with nature, give you? I believe that purity of your aura and energy flow outward, thus helping you to interact with the society and the environment better (as explained in diagram above).

Every aspect of our personal and professional life is a mind game, which you play to win mostly or retain the status quo. Mind games are seldom played to loose per se unless that are part of an overall bigger strategy. The overall mind game is displayed by your intentions, which are made public by the special communication code you choose to adopt.

Playing to win comes naturally not to all though everyone tries it. Only an exceptional leader retains that desire to succeed in every field of their personal or professional existence. The alpha specie (more importantly a successful person) exhibits certain quality traits in their desire to succeed such as self-actualization, focuss, intelligence, physically fit, mentally alert, empathetic, professionalism, knows his beans, willing to learn, is ambitious, has hunger to succeed, is a patient listener and most importantly communicates better.

The following questions need answers.

- Can you win without training your mind?
- Can you win by not practicing or testing new concepts?
- Can you win at all by playing the same game being played with same rules for hundred of years.

As times change, societies evolve, new ideas germinate, new consciousnesses evolve; we have to keep pace with change. James Redfield better writes nothing on subject of change, how we evolve, and can move forward than in his novel *The Celestine Prophecy.*

The book is a first-person narration of the narrator's spiritual awakening wherein the oriental spiritualism preponderates as he goes through a transitional period of his life. The book covered nine insights, later expanded to eleven insights, which the author saw in subsequent sequels. I will not cover the readable appeal but the various insights reflected are as under.

The First Insight: A new spiritual awakening occurs in human awakening brought about by spiritual unfolding.

The Second Insight: This awakening represents the creation of a new, more complete worldview, which replaces old preoccupation with survival and comfort.

The Third Insight: We live not in a material world, but in a world of dynamic energy. Humans have the ability to project energy by influencing other energy systems. It is possible to see this energy enveloping all living things.

The Fourth Insight: To gain energy, we tend to manipulate or force others to give us attention and thus energy. When we successfully dominate others in this way, we feel more powerful, leaving them weak to struggle for themselves. Competition for scarce human energy is the cause of all conflict between people.

The Fifth Insight: Insecurity and violence end when we experience connection with divine energy within. A sense of lightness or buoyancy along with the constant sensation of love are measures of this connection. If these measures are present, the connection is real; if not, it is only pretended.

The Sixth Insight: The more we stay connected, the more we are acutely aware of those times when we lose connection, usually when we are under stress. Stress is removable when you clear the past. This helps you to achieve your missions in life.

The Seventh Insight: Knowledge of our personal mission further enhances the flow of energy as we march toward our destinies. First, we have a question; then dreams, daydreams, and intuitions lead us towards the answers.

The Eighth Insight: We can increase the frequency of guiding coincidences by uplifting every person that comes into our lives. We need to be careful not to lose our inner connection when we have become part of romantic relationships. Uplifting others is especially effective in groups wherein each member can feel energy of all the others. With children, it is extremely important for their early security and growth. By seeing the beauty in every face, we lift others into their wisest self, and increase the chances of hearing a synchronic message.

The Ninth Insight: As we, all evolve toward the best completion of our spiritual missions; human focus on synchronic growth will fully automate the technological means of survival.

The Tenth Insight. The Tenth Insight is the realisation that throughout history, human beings have been struggling to achieve spirituality on earth. Each of us has personal goals and we have to perform particular tasks for the society. If we have a birth vision of what we wanted to accomplish in our lives then semantics of philosophy alone cannot cope with the common world vision.

The Eleventh Insight: The eleventh insight is the precise method through which we hold the vision. For centuries, religious scriptures, poems, and philosophies have pointed to a latent power of mind within all of us that mysteriously helps to affect what occurs in the future. Through this faith power, we can hold the vision of a spiritual world and build the energy in ourselves and in others to make this vision a reality.

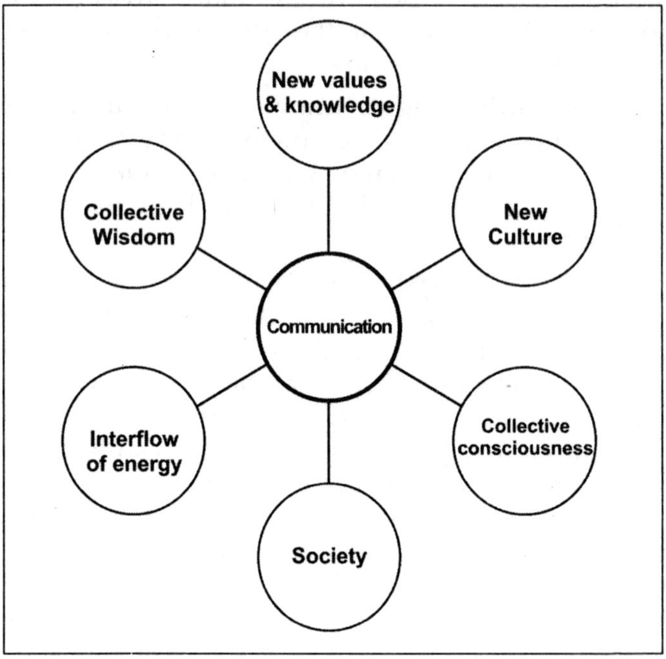

What I wanted to tell in the end was that the change in our lives is constant as the world moves to a new era of understanding and dealing with collective consciousness. In our own history we have had, Rama, Krishna, Buddha, Moses, Jesus, Muhammad, Gandhi, Martin Luther King etc and the list is endless. All spoke of new world and new leaders like them will definitely come forward repeatedly. All had one thing in common: magnetic connecting power with people of their idea and exhibited a communication excellence, which gave them more connectivity with others.

Let us glimpse into newer modules of enhancing your communication abilities by briefly glancing at more such concepts.

Internal Exploration

- Have you ever felt the need for spirituality to guide you in your life?
- Have you ever taken recourse to spiritual means to achieve something in life?
- Have you ever read any book or any piece that made you think different?
- If not, then better start doing it is never too late in life.

Chapter - 9

Hone Your Mind Better

"There are only two ways to live your life. One is as though nothing is a miracle. The other is as though everything is a miracle."

—Albert Einstein

In the study of sciences, which discourse on how mind controls your actions and thoughts and how one interacts with the environment, there has been quite a lot of progress in this field. The subject is age old and from the earliest recorded works the quest of humans how to control ones mind has never been unending. If one dwells into the sprituality of any sacred work of any religion, be it Geeta. Ramayana, Bible or Quran, all in their own ways teach the path of empowerment through practising mind control and your subsequent actions.

Latest studies of note which stand out to be reckoned with are in the psychological field of transactional analysis by Dr Berne and in particular the Karpman drama triangle, describe and examine mind games from a social and psychological perspective. Broadly, we use the term for any strategy or tactic where covert psychological manipulation or creation of coercive pressure of another person is a goal. He describes three roles or ego-states, the child, the parent, and the adult, and postulates that many negative behaviours traceable to switching or confusion of these ego-states, which have roots in rituals, and pastimes in social behaviour. The same is captured in the illustration below:

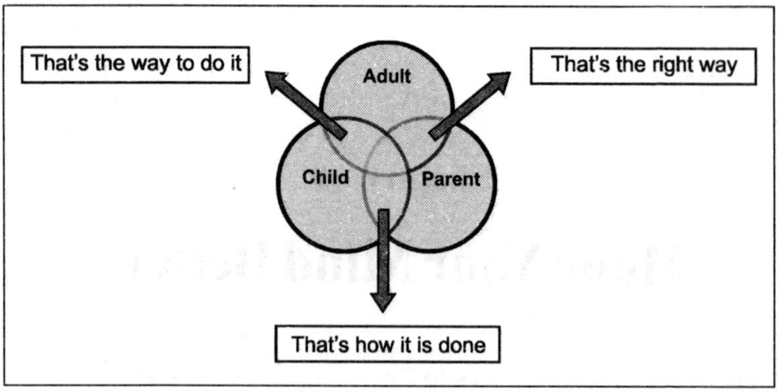

Many forms exhibit these states. A boss who talks to his staff as a controlling parent will often engender self-abased obedience. The responses from his employees can manifest also in terms of parent or like a child responses as mentioned above.

Whatever the explanation, it helps in understanding why and how the people behave, but always fall short of how to optimize the behaviour pattern for better communication. In early seventies a well-known linguist Richard Brandler and his professor Grinder did a thesis project in Santa Cruz, California. His prior job as interpreter in the US Army gave him insight into how others worked and performed and he made a basic model, which became as one of the primary tools of neurolinguistic programming. They sought to identify reasons, which made some persons so gifted despite everyone having different personalities. They both discovered some patterns that were quite similar. Thus, was born the concept of neuro-linguistic programming. (NLP)

NLP is defined as a quasi-spiritual behaviour modification (or performance psychology) technique. It is a study of the structure of subjective experience and a manual for structured use of creativity with the overall aim of enchasing performance.

The word NLP can be broken into three distinct segments: neuro, linguistic and programming. Neuro refers to the brain and its emanating signals, linguistics refer to the content, both verbal and non-verbal, programming is the way the content or signal is manipulated to convert it into useful information. NLP encompasses the ways in which people think and act in their day-to-day life and attempt to improve this aspect.NLP influences individuals in many ways in shaping their personality and behaviour patterns. For these spheres of change, see the figure given below:

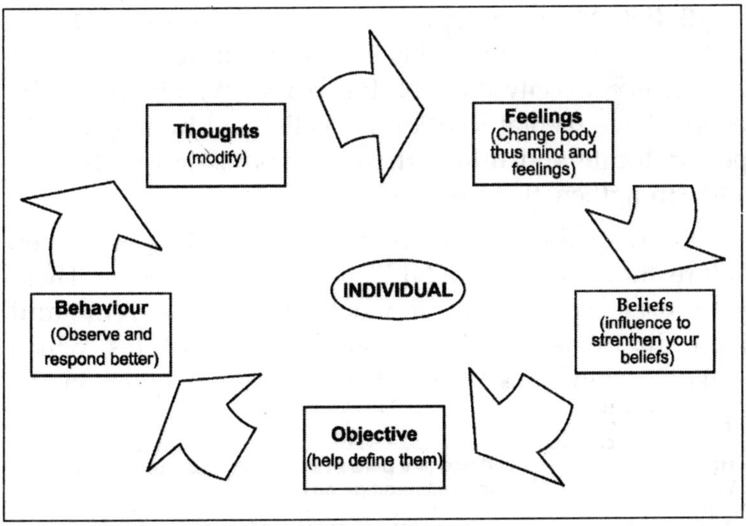

Objectives: Neurolinguistic programming helps define objectives in a way that makes them achievable. To do this NLP uses the well-informed outcomes technique.

Behaviour: Others can observe your behaviour. It is not possible to know someone's mind except when he expresses it. Both these aspects constitute behaviour. NLP works with behaviour, helping people observe and respond in useful ways.

Thoughts: The elements of thoughts involve seeing, hearing, having internal conversations, and experiencing sensations. NLP enables people to notice their thoughts and then if needed to modify them and thereby their experience.

Feelings: Are emotional responses or tendencies to respond. NLP as observed on activities of therapists and continues to emphasize on the importance of a balanced emotional state. It has techniques to manage emotions. NLP confirms psychosomatic relationship.

Belief: Means acceptance or something exists. Much of NLP is about change in beliefs, value attitudes as actual change occurs only then. NLP experts have observed that people have mental location for belief and by helping the person locate and utilize these it is possible to influence and strengthen their beliefs.

Many of the features of NLP existed long ago, even before they recognized NLP as a new discipline. There is, therefore, specific concoction between NLP and these disciplines. NLP has some specific features, which makes it stand out from others. These are given in the figure below :

Holistic approach	**All Parts of a person are interrelated and changes in one will impinge on others too.**
Focused on mental Processing	**How thoughts influence performance and offers ways of modifing mental patterns and helping people make changes to enhance their live.**
Utilizes specific Language Patterns	**A wide range of language process and patterns that can be applied in a variety of contexts.**
Work with conscious and unconscious mind	**Believes that unconscious mind has a powerful influence on our attributes and behaviour.**
Rapid in its process and results	**Brain works (and learns) speedily and therefore change can be brought about rapidly.**
Natural in approach	**Is a tool and not a prescription and is practitioner and client dependent.**

Training Model

Evolving a training model is essential before you can set your personal or your organizational training goals. Following are essential for evolving a training model.

- **Training outcomes**: A training brief should be prepared based on training need analysis, with outcomes (trainer, trainee, and organization) clearly identified and prioritised.
- **Identifying Trainees and Trainers:** Correct trainee and trainer identification is important both from organizational point of view as also for effectiveness in training. The diagram below gives guidelines for this.

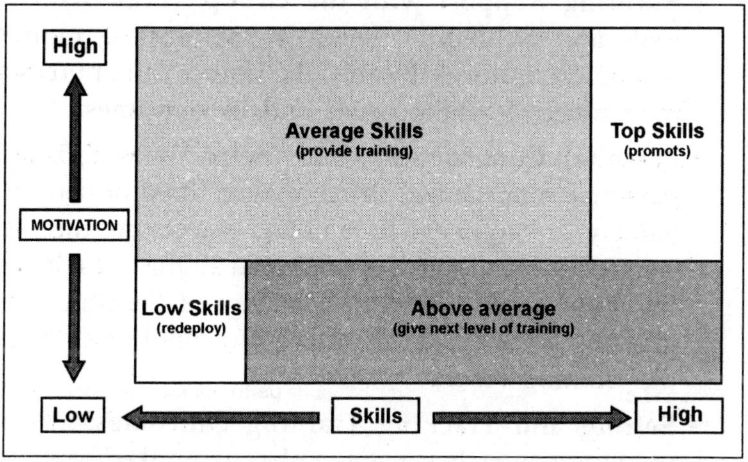

Designing the Structure. This involves working out the training syllabi in the manner which helps achieve your basic objectives as given below:

- Designing a syllabi for improving the effectiveness of both the organisation as well as the individual.
- Designing exercises.
- *Beliefs and Values.* NLP believes that the effect of training would be manifold if the values and beliefs

of the organisation, trainers and trainees are congruent with the system.

Training Techniques: There are a number of NLP training techniques, which make training more effective. These are as follows for ready reference.

- **Multiple Descriptions**: NLP emphasizes on the ability to see different viewpoints. These are your own, the trainees, the organisations and an impartial view that watches the entire enactment of the unfolding drama. Multiple descriptions give the trainer ability to make training three-dimensional by providing another alternative method to look at things.
- **Building Rapport with the Group**: NLP with its tools and techniques assists in establishing rapport among the trainees. By this, the trainer can appreciate the trainees learning needs and its outcomes.
- **Personal Congruence**: NLP helps in establishing personal congruence. It comprises three dimensions namely commitment to training, messenger-message congruence, and third, the personal alignment wherein the words voice and body language of the trainer, all give the same massage. More the congruence better the training result.
- **Setting and Tracking Training Outcomes:** Every teaching course has a slated objective linked to which are the outcomes of the course. Outcomes form the basic map for the trainer and need a closely tracking. A good trainer is aware of the outcomes and always relates it to the larger outcome.
- **Creating Resourceful Learning States in Participants.** A trainer needs to elicit states of learning and curiosity in the trainees. Once this is done, the trainees will give all their attention to the trainer and the teaching will become easier.

- **Unconscious Learning**: NLP stresses that learning is at two levels namely conscious and unconscious. Most courses engage the conscious attention of viewers. However, it is the latter, which is more important. NLP believes that training is about entertaining the conscious while at the same time teaching the unconscious. Teaching too much theory leaves the trainees knowing about the material but not very competent to do anything with it. Such should not be the outcome of good training.
- **Setting Frames:** Frames are crucial since they establish the filters through which the trainee interprets the material. For example, the frame (of mind) while reading a book, would be different from that of proofreading the errors. It is therefore essential for the trainer to set up contextual frames so that learning by trainees becomes easier.
- **Learning Styles:** Models of meta-programmes and metaphors are more effective. Meta-programmes are systematic and unconscious habitual ways of thinking. Its awareness helps the trainer to tailor material for different styles. Similarly, metaphors make the teaching more meaningful and interesting.
- **Future Pacing:** This NLP technique involves imagining oneself in a future time as a changed person due to the training undertaken. In this manner, the consequences of training can be realised and if required a correction made in one is learning.

Training Evaluation

The training evaluation should be systematic and continuous as in any mode or training programme. This establishes the need for what we have achieved and how far we need to travel further. Enhancing individual performance in training is one of the key factors of NLP exercises. It is achievable as follows:

- **Modelling:** This is a process where the emotional and physical characteristics of a person come close to the role model. By role modelling some of extremely capable people, it will be possible for us to see how much far we are in variance with them and thus take self corrective steps to enhance own potential.
- **Communication Congruence**: A large amount of interaction personal or interpersonal or inter or intra organisational takes place within the realms of day-to-day dealings. Here the clarity in communication can make the vital difference between success and failure. NLP propounds that communication is not merely saying but also truly feeling what is being spoken (congruence). It includes verbal as well as body signals.

NLP is primarily a self-improvement and a management tool. It guides a person to identify others, to modify one's own attitudes, emotions and thought processes to achieve excellence in his endeavours. This methodology sees a leader as a total person and proposes that a leader needs to be outcome oriented and has to adopt this as a way of life. It would entail raising your own standards by demanding more from yourself both professionally and in your personal life. Most of our thinking, including beliefs, subconsciously has a powerful effect on our behaviour. As soon as we change our behaviour, we communicate better to achieve our life goals.

This short journey into neo models of enhancing ones potential are just one of the various tools available. It's your own journey how you want to hone your mind, body, behaviour and subsequent actions so you can communicate better with the environment thus making you more effective as a person and a leader.

Internal Exploration

- Do you feel you have some deficiencies in you, which need correction?
- Have you ever worked out what precisely are those deficiencies in your character?
- Have you ever role modelled against a person to know where you actually stand?
- Have you ever thought of adopting techniques or taking corrective lessons to overcome your deficiencies?

Chapter - 10

Turbulence and Conniving

"A tail behind, a trunk in front,
Complete the usual elephant.
The tail in front, the trunk behind,
is what you very seldom find.
If you for specimens should hunt
With trunks behind and tails in front,
That hunt would occupy you long
The force of habit is so strong.
If you have always done it that way, it is probably wrong."

—AE Houseman

Let me break the monotony of the chapters and start this one with a humorous observation which I thought merited mentioning.

A young camel is asking her mother, "Mom can I ask you some questions which are troubling my mind". Obviously, the mother camel replied in affirmative. The young camel then asked, "Mom why we camels have a hump, flatfoot and hair covering our eyes". "Simple", said the mom, "hump is for storing water when we cross the waterless desert, flatfoot to stride firmly over the loose sands in the desert and hair to cover our eyes from the sands of the desert". "That's cool mom, a hump, flatfoot and hair over our eyes for living well in the desert, but what the hell are we doing in a Zoo".

The point I wish to make is that we can have the best of abilities, the best of tools, the best of everything you have ever dreamed off, but what is the use if you are at the wrong place at right time or vice versa.

I was reading something on the net, a post forwarded by a friend and this stuck in my mind.

- Smooth roads never make good drivers.
- Smooth seas never make good sailors.
- Clear skies never make good pilots.

Remember that a problem and hassle free life never makes a person strong.

We discussed that fact in our first chapter too. How did the genes survive and evolve? **Was their journey to be what we are today, simple or were they always tested by the elements of the nature?** Did the evolutionary genes give more than a fair fight to the harsh elements of nature and overcame them by conniving with the environment and mastering the art of surviving by constant and better mutation? Or they just sat back and let the harsh events overtake them?

Be strong enough to accept the challenges of life. Do not ask Life, "Why Me?" Instead, say, "Try me".

"The wisest mind has something yet to learn" should be our motto, regardless of age or wisdom

Well we were on subject of turbulence. Let me ask you a few very simple questions.

What would you do as a father or a caring parent when you see your physically fit child who is sleeping and lazing around? You would accept the situation or shake his lethargy.

- Will you not shake him?
- Will you not nudge him?
- Will you not talk to him?

Why as a parent do you feel obligated to do that? You do it for your child's good. Shaking the lethargy of your child would tantamount to turbulence because you are changing the situation of his natural lethargy. If you let anything live in its natural state of lethargy would you ever get, rose oil (by crushing roses), an iron rod (by smelting iron ore), a sparkling diamond (without polishing it). To get the best we need to change the status of natural things, we need to apply pressure and we need to cause turbulence.

Turbulent as a word is described in Oxford dictionary as disturbed, in commotion, restless, varying irregularly and its noun **turbulence** hence retains the same meaning.

Turbulence has a great communication meaning when applied to people and situations. I have seen this style of communication in defence services. We are familiar with bosses who on just taking over a new post practice the art of communicating through the mechanics of turbulence by:

- Change the existing situation.
- Change the style of functioning.
- Create a great flurry of activity.
- Show annoyance on the way things are moving.

What is the boss trying to achieve? Were the previous bosses so incompetent that they had not an iota of intelligence to perceive these things? The new boss is only shaking the dust off your shoulders. This mechanics of turbulence helps in reducing flab, re-looking at own policies, eliminating your inefficiencies, making you more responsive and infusing new ideas.

Here I do not want to sound out rightly outlandish by suggesting and inferring that turbulence in real life situation and the mechanics of conniving in the aspects of communication are two sides of the same coin. I know you will say how turbulence can be conniving. Let me explain it in a little more detail. What does the term conniving do, in the realms of communication? You are by conniving trying to achieve the following:

- Getting across the right message.
- Ensuring optimal execution of the task assigned.
- Eliminating inertia and initiating positive action.
- Inspiring confidence.
- Modifying the behaviour subtly.
- Applying the right kind of pressure.

Let us again go over a few examples of conniving as an art of communication, which I am sure you practice it unknowingly in everyday life.

Example 1: Manipulating the Need.

Mother to a child: "Come on teddy, my sweet teddy, you can watch your cartoons once you have finished your meal."

Example 2: Manipulating the Thought.

You want to migrate to America for better life, but what the hell are Americans doing in Indian companies?"

Example 3: Manipulating the Challenge.

Boss to group of juniors. "I am surrounded by bunch of idiots. Come here Tom; see what you can do about this task."

Example 4: Manipulating the Emotions.

"You love me and I am your heart, then trust me little one, let's do it this way."

Example 5: Manipulating the Mind.

"Only the best students of the college enter my tutorials gentlemen."

What do all the above examples tell you?

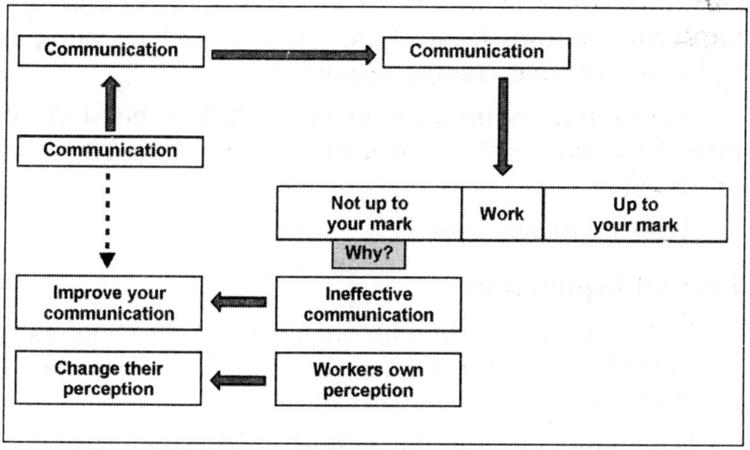

You are only manipulating the thoughts and resultant actions of others by an ulterior communication, which connives to meet your actual intent and desire.

We as individuals are what we are due to environmental factors. Have we not weathered all the storms and mutated to our best of what we are? Now not everyone can be an Alexander or Einstein, but we are what we are. Did our body, brain, mind, thoughts, did not connive with the prevailing interacting medium to be what you are? Our genes did to evolve to human species.

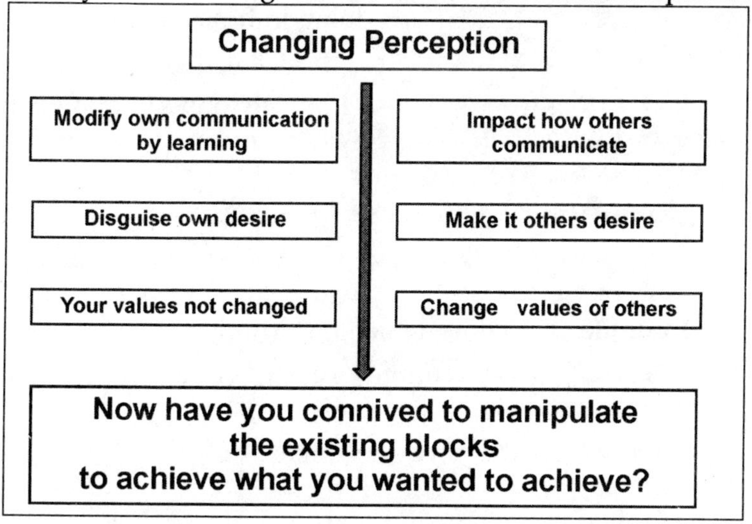

Our fathers taught us the art of survival. Your teachers imparted you knowledge. Then will you not be conniving to be an effective communicator?

Conniving communication also shakes the state of mental inaction, just as turbulence does it to a situation or an event.

Well I rest my case.

Internal Exploration

- Just think of people who changed the situation, as it existed before. What were the essential traits of their character?
- Have you ever had the courage to change a situation by your sheer perseverance?
- Has someone ever manipulated you to perform a task?
- Have you ever communicated with someone better to perform a particular task as per your original desires?

Chapter - 11

The Golden Sheen

"If I am to speak ten minutes, I need a week for preparation; if fifteen minutes, three days; if half an hour, two days; if an hour, I am ready now."

– ***Woodrow Wilson***

Well I have come to the end of my journey. Narrated below is the squeeze of all what I feel is communication all about. I have only a few simple things to say in the end.

- Be always open and honest.
- Throw out the correct intent always and every time.
- Smile.
- Trust others.
- Listen to others.
- Give your best.
- Have a big heart.
- Keep the message simple.
- Be confidant and articulate.
- Be open to thoughts, suggestions and ideas.
- Know your deficiencies.
- Correct the noticeable deficiencies by ardent self-control and continuous training.
- Stimulate your mind with new thoughts and keep it alive spiritually.

- Do whatever you do with full passion.
- Endow a positive attitude.
- Remember the failure is a learning curve and a key to the subsequent success.
- Never play God, for one you are not one, nor are the most knowledgeable.

Now I will try to put forth some stimulating quotes on communications subject as a whole and I call them **seven cardinal principles** of effective communications. They are:-

FIRST

"Speak when you are angry and you will make the best speech you will ever regret".

—Dr Lawerence J Peter

(NEVER LOOSE YOUR ANGER WHILE COMMUNICATING)

SECOND

"We have two ears and one mouth so that we can listen twice as much as we speak".

—Epictetus

(SO LISTEN MORE SPEAK LESS)

THIRD

"All noise is waste. So cultivate quietness in your speech, in your thoughts, in your emotions. Speak habitually low. Wait for attention and then your low words will be charged with dynamite".

—***Elbert Hubbard***

(SPEAK CALMLY AND CLEARLY IN MEASURED VOICE)

FOURTH

"Communication is depositing a part of yourself in another man".

—***Unknown***

(UNDERSTAND OTHERS AND EMOTE WITH THEM)

FIFTH

"First learn the meaning of what you say and then speak".

—***Epictetus***

(UNDERSTAND YOUR INNERSELF AND YOUR ABILITIES)

SIXTH

"Don't appear so scholarly, pray, humanize your talk and speak to be understood".

—***Moliere***

(BE OPEN, SIMPLE AND APPROACHABLE)

SEVENTH

"If you have nothing meaningful to say then keep quite".

—*Jesse*

With that, I end this book. I only hope you enjoyed reading it.

Index